W9-AHK-843

UPPER-ELEMENTARY
MEETINGS

Compiled by Group Books

Group Books

Loveland, Colorado

Upper-Elementary Meetings

Credits

Edited by Cindy Hansen
Designed by Judy Atwood Bienick
Cover photo by Brenda Rundback

Scripture quotations are from the Holy Bible, New International Version. Copyright © 1973, 1978, 1984 International Bible Society. Used by permission of Zondervan Bible Publishers.

Library of Congress Cataloging-in-Publication Data

Upper elementary meetings / compiled by Group Books; [edited by Cindy Hansen].
    p.   cm.
   ISBN 0-931529-86-7
   1. Church work with children. 2. Church group work with youth.
 I. Hansen, Cindy S.   II. Group Books (Firm)
   BV1475.2.U66 1989   89-32879
   268'.432—dc20   CIP

Printed in the United States of America

Contents

PART 1: MY FAITH

PART 2: MY SELF

PART 3: **MY RELATIONSHIPS**

Introduction

Why a book of upper-elementary programs? What's so hard about planning a roller-skating party, kite-flying contest or video night? That's what some adult sponsors from a Colorado church thought when they recently began an upper-elementary program.

They wanted programming ideas for the year, so they gave an anonymous interest-survey to their upper-elementary kids. The adult sponsors were expecting interests such as pizza nights, popcorn and movies, amusement park visits, and so on. The adults were jolted out of their preconceptions when the surveys were tallied. The kids' top five interests were:

★ Divorce

★ Death

★ Sex

★ Drugs

★ Losing a friend

Kids wanted time to ask questions about tough topics in a non-threatening atmosphere. Sure, the kids were interested in pizza nights, popcorn parties and other fun activities, but their top interests were these topics.

Upper-Elementary Meetings offers you and your upper-elementary kids 20 simple-to-follow meeting plans that address tough topics. The programs also combine fun and relaxation with music and refreshments. But they don't shy away from focusing on kids' concerns.

Use these meetings to fit your group's needs. If you're just beginning an upper-elementary group, take your own survey and discover the top interests. A survey could be as simple as listing all the topics covered in this book, then asking kids to choose the ones that interest them. Leave space for kids to add their own ideas for activities they'd like.

The meetings in *Upper-Elementary Meetings* are divided into the following sections:

★ **Introduction**—This section gives an overview and focuses on the topic.

★ **Objectives**—Each meeting lists several objectives that highlight facts kids will learn or activities they will participate in.

★ **Preparation**—All materials and preparations are listed. Try not to prepare everything by yourself. Involve the young people in preparing for the meeting and actually leading some activities. Upper-elementary kids can direct singing, lead a game or give directions for a craft project. Involve kids in prayers, scripture reading and role plays.

Also, involve parents or high school kids in your meetings. Just be careful not to overwhelm young people with an overload of adults. One adult per seven kids is plenty.

If a meeting contains especially sensitive areas, this section gives the leader hints on handling them.

★ **The Meeting**—This section contains step-by-step ideas and easy-to-follow instructions. Meetings start with an opening activity to get kids acquainted with each other and with the topic they'll discuss. Each meeting closes with a prayer, game, refreshments or other activity that wraps up and reinforces the lesson.

★ **Handouts**—All necessary handouts are included. You have permission to photocopy them for local church use.

Whether you use the meetings in this book for weekly get-togethers, retreats or lock-ins, use them to meet your kids' needs. And, have fun!

PART 1:

My Faith

By Tim Suby

Faith: Believing the Unbelievable

Many of today's young people have trouble believing in God. A lot of things seem unstable and bad to them. Even home life can often be hard to handle. Faith in a God who physically can't be seen, touched, heard, smelled or tasted is awfully tough for young people. In this meeting, kids will learn that we can have faith in God even though we can't see him directly.

Objectives

In this meeting, upper-elementary kids will:

★ hear about Jesus' life and miracles;
★ explore what faith means;
★ see how Daniel had to take a real "leap of faith"; and
★ show what God has done for them.

Preparation

Read the meeting. Gather masking tape, a gossip newspaper or magazine, and two signs (one labeled "True" and one labeled "False"). Each young person will need a marker and a 2×10 inch strip of paper.

Print the headlines from activity #1 onto the newspaper or magazine. Tape the "True" and "False" signs on opposite sides of the room. Practice reading "In the Den," making sure you leave pauses for kids to do actions and sounds.

The Meeting

 **1 Extra! Extra!** Pull out your gossip newspaper or magazine and tell the kids that just for fun you're going to read a few headlines. Read one or two actual headlines and say: Can you believe this stuff? Do they actually expect us to believe this just because they wrote it?

Explain to the group that you're going to read several

more headlines. Tell the kids that after you read each headline, they are to stand near the "True" sign or the "False" sign, according to whether or not they think the headline is truthful.

Read the following headlines (omit the parenthetical information), interspersing them with real headlines from the newspaper or magazine:

★ Stretch Your Grocery Dollar With Incredible Meal Plan Called "How to Feed a Multitude With a Minimal Amount of Food" (Jesus feeds the 5,000—John 6:5-13)

★ Miraculous Rescue at Sea! Man Saves Lives of His Friends by Yelling at the Storm to Stop. And It Does! (Jesus calms the storm—Mark 4:37-41)

★ Blind Since Birth, He Receives His Sight Through Mud (Jesus heals a blind man—John 9)

★ Religious Leader Jailed, Tortured and Executed Only Five Days After City Celebrated His Return (Jesus arrested, tortured and killed—Luke 22—23)

★ What a Reunion! Dead Teacher Visits Amazed Students (Jesus visits the disciples—John 20:19-23)

After you're done, say: I can tell you that at least five of these stories are true.

Reveal to the group which headlines were about events in Jesus' life. Discuss these questions:

★ Why were some of the headlines easier to believe than others?

★ Why are stories about Jesus sometimes hard to believe?

★ Just because things are printed in newspapers or magazines, do we believe them? Why or why not?

★ Just because things are printed in the Bible, do we believe them? Why or why not?

2 Leap of faith

Say: In Hebrews it says, "Now faith is being sure of what we hope for and certain of what we do not see." We're going to try and experience the meaning of this passage.

Pair kids with a partner who's close to their same size. Have one person in each pair stand with arms crossed and knees locked. The other person stands about one foot behind his or her partner. Say to the partners in front: You are to fall back without bending your knees or moving your feet. Your partner will stop your fall and push you back up. Have faith! Trust that your partner will catch you.

Do this two or three times, then switch.

Ask: Which was harder: falling or catching? Why?

Say: The people falling always hoped their partner would catch them even though they couldn't see them. As Christians, we have faith that God will catch us whenever we fall, even though we can't see him.

3 In the den

Say: We're now going to hear about Daniel who had to make a real leap of faith. But his leap wasn't just to the floor; it was into the mouths of lions. I'll read the story and you'll respond at different words.

Divide the group into four groups and assign each small group one of these responses:

★ **Daniel**—Point to the sky and say, "I'll always trust God."

★ **King**—Snap fingers and say, "Here comes the king. Here comes the king."

★ **Administrators**—Sneer and say, "We despise Daniel."

★ **Lions**—Rub hands together and say, "It's dinner time."

Have groups practice their responses. Encourage kids to "ham it up" as you read the story on page 12. Pause for responses everywhere you see the ellipsis (. . .).

4 Headlines

After you've read the story, ask: If we were to write a headline for a gossip newspaper or magazine about Daniel, what would it be? Maybe something like this: "Lions' Mouths Mysteriously Closed While Man Walks Around in Their Cage."

Let kids describe some other headline ideas.

Hand out a strip of paper and a marker to each person. Then have the kids get in the same pairs as in activity #2. Explain to the pairs that they are to write two headlines that have to do with faith. For example: "God Loves Kids, Even Though They Disobeyed Parents." When kids are finished, tape headlines on the wall for all to see.

5 Headline prayer

Form a half-circle facing the headlines. Explain that for a closing prayer the group will thank God for what he has done. Have them pray silently as you insert a few of the headlines into the prayer. Pray: Dear God, thank

In the Den

Now in the time when Darius was the king . . . he appointed 120 men to be the administrators . . . of the land. Now these administrators . . . were supervised by Daniel . . . The administrators . . . hated Daniel . . . because he made sure they did their jobs honestly and right. The administrators . . . watched for Daniel . . . to fail at his job or do something dishonestly, but Daniel . . . was honest and trustworthy. So the administrators . . . said, "We will never find any way of getting rid of Daniel . . . because of his work. The only way we will get rid of him will have to be because of the law of his God."

So the administrators . . . went as a group to the king . . . and said, "Oh, king . . . Darius, live forever. We think that since you are such a great king . . . that everyone in all the land should pray to you for the next 30 days. If anyone prays to another god or man, they should be thrown into the lions' . . . den. Please write that into a law, oh king . . ."

The king . . . was so flattered that he did just that. And the administrators . . . were excited because they had found a way to get rid of Daniel . . . for good.

Now when Daniel . . . heard about this law, he went home to his room to pray to the living God, because he was troubled by this law. Daniel . . . knew that it would break God's law to pray and worship another man or god, even if it was the king . . .

As Daniel . . . was praying, the administrators . . . came to his house and saw him. They grabbed Daniel . . . and took him before the king . . . They said, "Oh king . . . here is Daniel . . . who is mocking your law by praying to a god who is not you. Enforce your law, oh king . . ."

Now the king . . . was very sad, because he liked Daniel . . . quite a lot, and knew that Daniel . . . was one of his best men. But the king . . . knew that not even a king . . . could ignore a law being broken. So he sadly gave the order to have Daniel . . . thrown into the lions' . . . den. He said to Daniel, . . . "May your God whom you faithfully serve, rescue you."

So Daniel . . . was thrown into the lions' . . . den. A large stone was placed on top and the king . . . sealed it himself—much to the administrators' . . . delight.

The next day the king . . . ran to the lions' . . . den and sadly called out, "Daniel . . . servant of the living God, whom you serve faithfully, has your God saved you?"

Much to the king's . . . delight, Daniel . . . answered, "Oh king . . . live forever! My God has sent his angel, and he shut the mouths of the lions . . . The lions . . . have not hurt me, because I was found innocent in God's sight. Nor have I ever wronged you, oh king . . ."

The king . . . was overjoyed and ordered Daniel . . . to be brought out of the lions' . . . den. And when Daniel . . . was brought out of the lions' . . . den, no wound was found on him, because he had faith in his God.

Now the king . . . was angry with the administrators . . . who had tried to have Daniel . . . killed. So the king . . . ordered the administrators . . . to be thrown into the lions' . . . den. Much to the lions' . . . delight, because they were very hungry.

So Daniel . . . prospered during the reign of king . . . Darius.

you for all you've done for us. And thank you for people like Daniel who showed what faith is all about. We have faith that you'll always (insert headlines here; for example, "Forgive us"). We ask that you help us always to be faithful to you. Amen.

Meeting 2

By Terry Vermillion

We Are the Church

In a busy life where many church activities divide families—parents go to one room for an activity, children go to another room—this meeting involves parents and upper-elementary children together. This meeting gives families a fun, active, entertaining introduction to the church. Families learn:

★ we are the church;
★ we are the family of God; and
★ we are called to love one another.

Objectives

In this meeting, upper-elementary kids and their parents will:

★ rotate to various stations and learn about communion, baptism, teaching, preaching and reaching out;
★ mold clay to symbolize their family;
★ make a bookmark to remind them to reach out;
★ search the church directory for ideas of good teachers; and
★ thank God for their church and for a chance to worship together.

Preparation

Read the meeting and prepare materials as described for each of the five stations. Place the materials at each station as needed. Prepare a posterboard sign for each of the stations. Photocopy the station descriptions and glue each one to the corresponding posterboard sign.

Tape the signs to the walls at various places in the room. After each family finishes a station, the members must tape one end of a piece of yarn on that station's sign and then tape the other end of the yarn to the next station's sign. All families will complete a web of yarn around the entire room after they've completed the five stations. Cut enough pieces of yarn for each family to have five. Make the

pieces long enough to reach from station to station.
Adapt the stations to fit your church's basic beliefs.

The Meeting

 1 Sing a song and get along Gather the families in a circle and sing familiar songs such as "We Are the Family of God" from *Songs* (Songs and Creations). Sing another song to introduce each other, such as "Jesus Loves Me." Instead of singing "Jesus loves me, this I know," sing names in place of the word "me." For example, "Jesus loves Dave, this we know . . ."

Divide the group into five smaller groups, keeping families together. If you have fewer than five families, assign each one to a station. Say: Today we're going to discover some of God's ideas for his church. We are the church. We are God's family. He wants us to love each other. He gives us several ways to do this: communion, baptism, preaching, teaching and reaching out. Because God loves us, we love each other.

 2 Family stations The families will have five minutes to complete the activity at each station. The instructions are written on each station's posterboard sign. When it's time to rotate to the next station, signal by singing "Jesus Loves Me." Families then tape one end of a piece of yarn to the posterboard sign and the other end of the yarn to the next posterboard sign. They move clockwise from station to station.

3 A web of yarn As families finish their fifth station, have them gather in the center of the room within the web of yarn. Say: We've woven a bond of love through our local church and each of us has done our part. If some group had not done its part we would have no web. If someone would walk out now, he or she would break the web. In the church, we need to love each other. We need to gather for strength. We need to continually renew the bond of love. So if we're going to reach out to the world in love, we need to take part in sharing and serving, baptism, teaching, preaching and reaching out.

Wrap up your session with a prayer, thanking God for your church and for the chance to worship together. Ask everyone to join you in silent prayer as you pray.

Then say: We now send you out of this bond of love into the world. I'll cut the yarn and as you pass through the bond, each of you will receive a piece of yarn to wear. Wear it now as you leave, and wear it to church on Sunday to remind you to spread God's love to those who weren't here today.

Cut the yarn and give a piece to each person as he or she leaves.

Each family will need a Bible, marker, piece of newsprint, pitcher of water, packet of pre-sweetened Kool-Aid, spoon, cups, cookies, tape and yarn.

Station #1 (Communion)

Instructions: Ask someone to read the first paragraph. Then ask someone to read the scripture. Follow the instructions and complete the station.

"Many churches' beliefs about communion vary. But communion is a time for sharing with our immediate family, with our church family, and with Jesus and the communion of saints. This sharing with each other goes on not just in worship, but all of the time. We serve each other in our church as well as outside of the church, just as Jesus and his disciples served others."

1. Read 1 Corinthians 11:23-26.

2. Take a marker and write on the sheet of newsprint one way you can serve other people in the church. For example, help fold bulletins, pick up a homebound person and bring him or her to church, sit near a visitor and answer questions about the church.

3. Take a pitcher of water and a packet of Kool-Aid mix. Have one person stir the water gently. Watch it swirl in the pitcher. Now add the drink mix and stir gently. Can you separate the drink mix from the water? Jesus is like that. He mixes so completely with our lives that we can't separate him from our actions. We want to do what God wants us to do because Jesus is a part of us—like the drink mix is a part of the water.

4. Serve the drink and cookies to each person in your group. As you eat the cookies, tell one way you have helped another person this week. Enjoy the snack.

5. When you hear the signal, tape one end of the yarn to this station's sign and tape the other end to the next station's sign.

Station #2 (Baptism)

Instructions: Ask someone to read the first paragraph. Then ask someone to read the scriptures. Follow the instructions and complete the station.

"Baptism is a sign of faith. It shows that we are a part of the church, the family of God. When people are baptized, our church family promises to teach them and care for them."

1. Read Romans 6:3-4; and 1 John 3:1.

2. Distribute a handful of clay to each person. Create yourself in clay. Make the lump of clay look as much like you as possible.

3. Pretend the box is the church. Put together a family group, just like your family, entering the little church. Talk about your baptism. When and where were you baptized? How did you learn about God? Did your family teach you? Did a friend teach you? How can a family help each other continue to grow as children of God?

4. When you hear the signal, tape one end of the yarn to this station's sign and tape the other end to the next station's sign.

Each family will need a Bible, cardboard box, piece of yarn and tape. Each family member will need a handful of clay.

Each family will need a Bible, yarn, tape, piece of paper and a pencil. You'll also need one pictorial church directory or a listing of church members in this station.

Station #3 (Teaching)

Instructions: Ask someone to read the first paragraph. Then ask someone to read the scriptures. Follow the instructions and complete the station.

"The church contains many members of varying talents and interests. Some people are preachers, some are teachers, some are musicians, and so on. But church is a place for all people to read the Bible together and learn more about Jesus."

1. Read 1 Corinthians 12:5-6, 28; and Ephesians 4:11.

2. Look at the church directory. Pretend you're a volunteer coordinator and choose one teacher for each of these groups: preschool, grade school, junior high, high school, and adult.

3. Explain your choices. Write the names and the reasons for choosing them on the paper. Fold the paper and leave it by the posterboard sign.

4. When you hear the signal, tape one end of the yarn to this station's sign and tape the other end to the next station's sign.

Station #4 (Reaching Out)

Instructions: Ask someone to read the first paragraph. Then ask someone to read the scripture. Follow the instructions and complete the station.

"We come to church to hear the good news of Jesus' Death and Resurrection. We learn lessons in Sunday school and we hear preaching in worship. Then we go out into the world, helping others and telling everyone the good news."

1. Read Matthew 28:18-20.

2. Distribute the art supplies. Have everyone make a construction paper bookmark as a reminder to reach out, help others and spread the good news. For example, draw a man shouting, "Good News!" and another person with her hand by her ear listening.

3. Cover the bookmarks with clear plastic and trim to fit.

4. Describe the bookmarks. Take them home as reminders to reach out to others.

5. When you hear the signal, tape one end of the yarn to this station's sign and tape the other end to the next station's sign.

Each family will need a Bible, yarn, tape, scissors, construction paper, markers and adhesive clear-plastic shelf covering.

Each family will need a Bible, yarn and tape.

Station #5 (Preaching)

Instructions: Ask someone to read the first paragraph. Follow the instructions and complete the station.

"Our church has someone special to help us build a bond of love. Our pastor has been specially called by God and trained to guide us. One of the pastor's jobs is to explain the gospel to people of all ages. But the pastor is not the only one who is called to spread the Word. We are too."

1. Divide into two smaller groups. Each group should choose one of the following parables and retell it in a modern-day style. Try to retell the stories as you would to a person who's never heard them before.

★ Luke 15:11-32 (the prodigal son). For example: "There was a man who had two sons. The younger son said, 'Dad. I'm 18 now. Give me half of the family's money so I can go out on my own. I want out of here.' The man sadly did as his son asked. His son went traveling across the country. He wasted the money on drugs, alcohol and prostitutes . . ."

★ Matthew 25:1-13 (the foolish maidens). For example: "The kingdom of heaven can be compared to 10 families who were preparing for the day their children would attend college. All 10 families set up savings accounts. Five families were foolish; five were wise. The foolish ones failed to put money into the accounts on a steady basis. They thought, 'We'll do it next month,' but they never did. The wise families faithfully invested a certain amount of money each month . . ."

2. Retell the stories. Discuss spreading the good news to others.

3. When you hear the signal, tape one end of the yarn to this station's sign and tape the other end to the next station's sign.

By Terry Vermillion

Called Children of God

Sleeping Dog was named by his father. Born in the hunger moon when the camp dogs spent most of their time sleeping in sheltered places, Sleeping Dog seemed a good name for the sleeping baby. When Sleeping Dog had lived 12 winters, he went into the forest for his time alone before joining the men in the hunting lodge. He slept in the branches of a tree while a pack of wolves slept below him. In the morning they had vanished. When he returned to the village and told his story, he was given a new name. He was called Sleeping Wolf.

There's a time in our lives when we're called by a new name. When we're baptized, we're identifying ourselves as part of the church, the children of God. We make it known that we are now "Christian," our new name as a member of God's family.

Objectives

In this meeting, upper-elementary kids will:
★ recognize each group member's accomplishments;
★ appreciate more of the Native American culture; and
★ see baptism as a significant change in life.

Preparation

Read the meeting. Gather 3×5 cards, paper, markers, paste, blackboard and chalk (or newsprint and markers), and a Bible or Bible story book. Photocopy the "Indian Sign Language" and "Pictographs of Indian Names" handouts.

You'll divide the group into tribes for the first activity. To do this, prepare a 3×5 card for each student. Draw or paste a copy of a tribe symbol to each card. (See the "Pictographs of Indian Names" handout.) Make similar cards for the small groups you want. For example, if you have 16 children, make four copies of four different symbols so that there will be four tribes of four children each.

Ask high school kids to pantomime the stories in activity #2 as you read them. The World Book Encyclopedia gives the origins of many famous Indian names. You can also create your own stories such as the one at the beginning of this meeting.

The Meeting

1· Visiting tribes

As children arrive, give them each a 3×5 pictograph card and tell them to gather in a group with everyone who has the same symbol. Have each tribe sit Indian-style (legs crossed) in a circle. Give each tribe a copy of the "Indian Sign Language" handout. Demonstrate a few signs and have the children try to sign them. Demonstrate signing a question and see who can guess what you've asked. Give them a few minutes to try the signs within their tribe.

Explain that they're peaceful Indians preparing to visit another tribe in their nation. Have them prepare one question to ask the other tribe; for example, "Are you a friend?" Allow a few minutes for tribes to prepare a question. You may want to offer suggestions if a tribe can't make up a question.

Designate one-half of the tribes as visiting tribes and the other half as home tribes. Have each visiting tribe visit a home tribe and ask their question in sign language. Caution them that there's to be no talking. They're to use only signs. Have the home tribe answer the question in sign language. When the first question has been answered, have the home tribe question the visiting tribe. Give tribes the opportunity to be both home tribes and visiting tribes. Have the tribes visit as many other tribes as time allows, or as kids' interest level permits. Instruct adults to let the tribes struggle with the sign language, but be ready to step in with hints if a tribe is completely baffled.

2 Naming ceremony

Gather the children into one circle. Read aloud the story of Jesus' Baptism from Matthew 3:13-17 or from a Bible story book. Say: At Jesus' Baptism, we heard God call him by a new name, "Son of God," for the first time in his life on Earth. Our new name, "child of God," or "Christian," which we announce at baptism, shows we're different because we've accepted God's call to be a part of his family. The Indians received a new name because the tribe saw a change in them.

Ask the high school kids to act out the following stories while you or another person read them.

Pocahontas

Pocahontas, the daughter of Powhatan, was fascinated by the English settlers at Jamestown. She'd watch from the trees while the settlers built their houses. Captain John Smith claimed that she saved him from being killed by the Indians and convinced her father to be friends with the settlers. In 1613, the settlers captured Pocahontas during an Indian fight and held her captive on an English ship in the harbor. She was still fascinated by the English and tried to learn their customs. While she was captive, she fell in love with Englishman John Rolfe and was married to him in 1614. She realized that the Christianity followed by the English was a powerful religion, and she believed in Christ. She took the name Rebecca to symbolize her change to Christianity.

Sitting Bull

His name was Slow. Everything he did as a child he did slowly and with careful thought. Some of the tribe thought he was slow in the head.

When he was in his teens his father, Sitting Bull, gave him a coup (pronounced koo) stick. The Sioux Indians thought the bravest thing an Indian could do was to sneak up on an enemy in a battle, touch the enemy with the coup stick, and then ride away without harming the enemy or getting injured himself. The man who would let his enemy live to attack another day was brave indeed.

When a war party left camp to chase their old enemy, the Crows, Slow sneaked out and followed them. During the fight, Slow raced in on his pony, hit a Crow warrior with his coup stick and raced away. That night an older warrior told the story at campfire. Slow's father was so proud of his son that he gave Slow his own name. From then on Slow was known as Sitting Bull and his father changed his own name to Jumping Bull.

Red Jacket

Red Jacket received his name as an adult. He made friends with some British soldiers. One of them gave him the coat from a British soldier's uniform, the famous Red Coat that the British wore when they later fought the Revolutionary War. From that time on, he could be seen hunting or leading war parties in the red coat and was called Red Jacket.

Next, say: Many things have happened since you were born to change you from a baby to what you are today. You may have worked to become a good soccer player, or you may have found a place you like to visit or you may have a skill such as making friends. Choose a person sitting close to you and decide on a new name that tells something about him or her; for example, "Soccer Ball," "Friendly" or "Canary Owner." Remember this isn't a time to be silly, but a time to express positive things about each person.

3 Pictographs
Join in one large circle and have partners introduce each other by their new names. Give each person a piece of paper and markers. Distribute the "Pictographs of Indian Names" handout; then illustrate on the blackboard or newsprint how some Indians express a name in pictographs. Have kids each draw their new name as a pictograph.

4 Thank you for friends
Have the kids stand in one large circle. Ask each person to lay his or her pictograph in the center of the circle so that everyone can see it. Read aloud 1 John 3:1-3. Then use sign language to pray, "Thank you for friends." Have everyone practice, then sign the prayer together.

5 Snack time
Sign, "We eat." Serve a food that carries out the Indian theme, such as Indian Fry Bread. Indian Fry Bread is a flat bread that is cooked in hot oil. For a quick version, take canned biscuits and roll them with a rolling pin until they are about eight inches in diameter. Fry in about one-half inch of cooking oil in a heavy skillet, turning once until lightly browned. Remove from skillet and pat off extra grease with paper towels. Serve warm or cold with honey or butter.

If you live in a corn-growing area, check farmers' markets in the fall for popcorn that's still on the cob. The children can remove the corn from the cob for popping. Other Indian snacks you could serve are beef jerky, dried fruit or blue tortillas with butter.

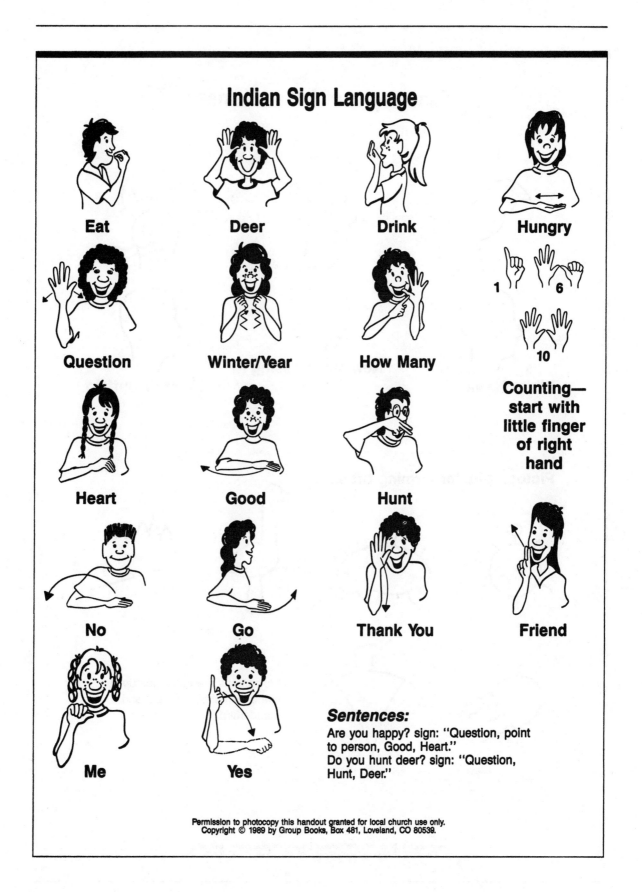

Indian Sign Language

Eat · Deer · Drink · Hungry

Question · Winter/Year · How Many

1 · 6 · 10

Counting—start with little finger of right hand

Heart · Good · Hunt

No · Go · Thank You · Friend

Me · Yes

Sentences:
Are you happy? sign: "Question, point to person, Good, Heart."
Do you hunt deer? sign: "Question, Hunt, Deer."

Pictographs of Indian Names

White Hawk

New Moon Rising

Roaring Buffalo

Pictographs for forming tribes

Pictographs are turtle, porcupine, crane, campfire, live bear and thunderbird.

By Dr. Scott E. Koenigsaecker

Lead Us Not Into Temptation

Oscar Wilde once said, "I can resist anything except temptation." A week, a day, an hour in the day does not pass without something or someone tempting us— enticing us to act opposite the way God wants us to act. We have four basic responses to temptation:

★ We can give in to the temptation;
★ We can resist it;
★ We can try to wish it away; or
★ We can underestimate it.

What do we do when we are tempted? How should we respond? Use this meeting to help young people understand temptation, as well as learn how to deal effectively with it when it strikes.

Objectives

In this meeting, upper-elementary kids will:

★ play an opening game that tempts them to do some wild and crazy things;
★ make collages of temptations;
★ discuss four stages of temptation;
★ explore three principles to deal more successfully with temptation; and
★ affirm Jesus' forgiveness of our sins.

Preparation

Read the meeting. Gather Bibles, magazines, construction paper, glue, scissors, "Let's Go Fishing" and "Getting a Grip on Temptation" handouts, pencils, a fishing pole, fish crackers, refreshments, and candy or fruit for rewards.

Divide the group into four teams by making fish-shape name tags of different colors—red, yellow, blue, green. Distribute them randomly as kids enter the meeting area.

Read activity #1 and get four leaders to oversee each temptation task. You'll need a whistle or other noisemaker to signal when it's time to rotate to another exercise.

Ask a person to role play the fisherman in activity #3.

The Meeting

1 I dare you

Give kids each a different-color name tag. Ask them to find everyone with the same-color tag and form a group. Once with their group, have kids each tell one thing they learned this week.

Say: We're going to learn some more at this meeting. We're going to learn about temptation.

Assign each group to an adult or high school student. Give the leaders candy or fruit with which to reward the participants after they complete each task.

Explain to the kids that they'll have two minutes to do the assigned task. If they complete each one, they'll receive a wonderful reward. Have them rotate clockwise to the next task when the whistle blows. Here are the tasks:

★ *Temptation Task #1*—Everyone stands on his or her head and sings the alphabet song—"A-B-C-D . . ."

★ *Temptation Task #2*—Everyone does the bicycle exercise (lie on back, put feet in air and pedal). Anyone who knows the song and sings "A Bicycle Built for Two," wins an extra reward.

★ *Temptation Task #3*—Form a pyramid and recite, "Peter Piper Picked a Peck of Pickled Peppers" as fully as possible.

★ *Temptation Task #4*—Everyone jogs in place and counts to 50. Afterward, they sit down and say, "Whew. What a day."

After everyone has given in to temptation to do the crazy tasks, ask:

★ What did you think was the "craziest" tempting task?

★ What tempted you to complete each station?

Say: I could tell that many of you were tempted by the rewards to complete the tasks. My suspicion is that without the rewards very few of you would have (mention the craziest thing you had them do here). This game illustrates an important point about life. There are many things we don't think we'd ever do, yet we find ourselves doing them. Why do we do them? We do them because we are tempted by their rewards. The rewards of power, pleasure and money motivate us to do all kinds of things we really don't want to do. Temptation is a normal part of life. Ignoring it doesn't make it go away. So during this meeting, we're going to look at the tempting subject of temptation, discover how to recognize the warning signs and learn how to respond.

2 Life is tempting

Give each small group magazines, construction paper, glue and scissors. Have each group make a "Temptation Creation" collage. Instruct students to cut out pictures or words to represent temptations in their lives. Once each group has completed its collage, have each student in the group share what he or she contributed and why. Then select a spokesperson from each group to tell about the group's "Temptation Creation." Hang the collages on one wall in the shape of a "T"—for "Temptation."

3 Let's go fishing

Gather in a large group. Ask the volunteer you chose before the meeting to role play the following fisherman fable:

Have the volunteer pick up a fishing pole and say: "How many of you have ever fished? Catching fish isn't always easy. The secret to being a good fisherman, they tell me, is to know 'where' the fish are biting and 'what' the fish are biting. Once you've found a good spot, all you have to do is bait your hook with the right stuff and the rest will take care of itself. This looks like a great spot, so I guess I'm ready to bait my hook and catch some big fish." Pantomime baiting the hook, or try baiting your hook with a big, juicy worm! Once you have baited your hook, toss your baited hook into the "water." Act as though you've caught a big fish. Reel it in and land it, put down your pole, slap your hands together, and say: "Easy isn't it? Being tempted to sin is like being fished for. Like a fisherman, sin throws the baited hook of temptation right into the river of our life. Like a fish, we see the temptation, swim as fast as we can to catch it, bite into it, and discover a big sharp surprise. Once we're hooked by our actions, we find that there's little we can do—sin just reels us in and lands us. And once we are landed . . . well, it's the big frying pan of life for us." (Sigh and exit.)

After the fisherman leaves, ask kids to go back to their

small groups. Give each group member a "Let's Go Fishing" handout and a pencil. Review the four steps of temptation as role played by the fisherman and as stated on the handout:
★ Seeing the hook;
★ Being attracted to the bait;
★ Thinking of possible choices; and
★ Taking action (action can either hook you to the temptation, or action can take you away from the temptation).

Assign each small group one situation from the handout. The members are to read their tempting situation aloud and identify the steps of temptation. For example, in the first situation, the tempting hook is the smart kid's test right in front of you. The attraction is the desire to get a good grade and make your parents proud. Possible actions could be cheating by looking at the test or not cheating and keeping your eyes on your own paper. One action hooks you into sin, the other action leads you away from the temptation.

Allow 10 minutes for small groups to complete their handout. Then discuss the answers as a large group. Award each group member a fish cracker for thinking through these tempting situations.

4. Getting a grip
Explain three principles about temptation:
★ *Principle #1*—Temptation happens to everyone.
★ *Principle #2*—We're never tempted beyond our limits. God helps us cope when temptation becomes more than we can handle.
★ *Principle #3*—God always provides an escape route from temptation. We have to be willing to look for it and use it.

Distribute the "Getting a Grip on Temptation" handout and a Bible to each person. Make sure everyone has a pencil. Say: Here are three scrambled messages for you to decode. The messages tell you more about these principles. You'll also find a promise of forgiveness for times we fail. God loves us no matter what. Work with a partner if you want to.

Give the kids several minutes to decode the messages. Then read the messages to reaffirm that God is with us through tempting times. He gives us strength to withstand temptation.

5 Tempting the tastebuds
Use one of these tempting desserts for refreshments:

★ Ask the adult sponsors to form a serving line of goodies, such as ice cream, fruit, cookies, Jell-O or pudding. See if the adults can tempt kids to take the items they're serving. Kids can only choose one item.

★ Carry out the fishing concept by having students "fish" for their dessert. Students can line up and put a fishing line behind a short wall (made out of cardboard or out of a sheet). A person behind the wall attaches a candy bar or other dessert on the line to be reeled in. A "pond of punch" or "river of root beer" could accompany the treats.

Let's Go Fishing

Instructions: Read your assigned tempting situation, then answer the questions.

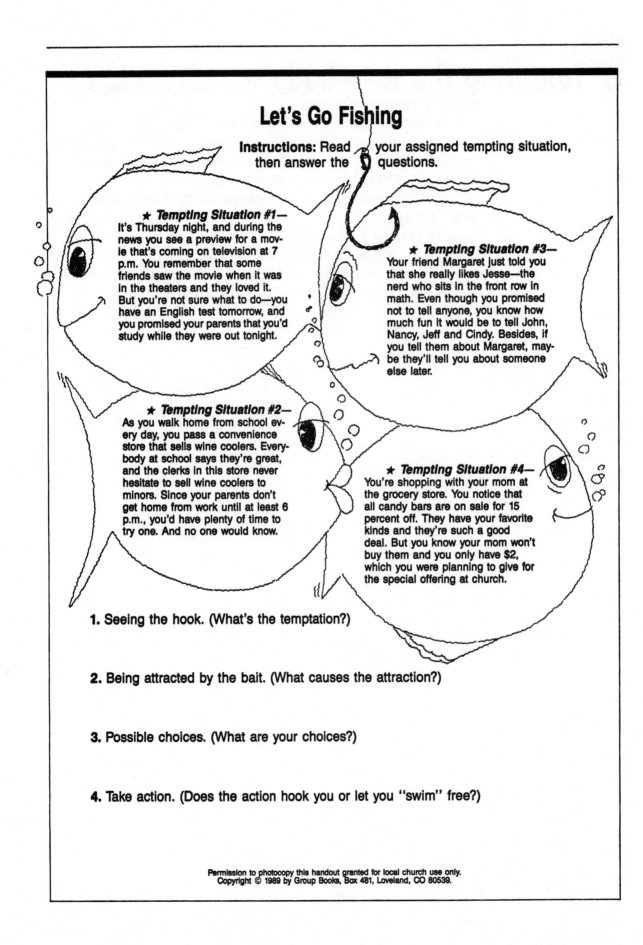

★ Tempting Situation #1—
It's Thursday night, and during the news you see a preview for a movie that's coming on television at 7 p.m. You remember that some friends saw the movie when it was in the theaters and they loved it. But you're not sure what to do—you have an English test tomorrow, and you promised your parents that you'd study while they were out tonight.

★ Tempting Situation #2—
As you walk home from school every day, you pass a convenience store that sells wine coolers. Everybody at school says they're great, and the clerks in this store never hesitate to sell wine coolers to minors. Since your parents don't get home from work until at least 6 p.m., you'd have plenty of time to try one. And no one would know.

★ Tempting Situation #3—
Your friend Margaret just told you that she really likes Jesse—the nerd who sits in the front row in math. Even though you promised not to tell anyone, you know how much fun it would be to tell John, Nancy, Jeff and Cindy. Besides, if you tell them about Margaret, maybe they'll tell you about someone else later.

★ Tempting Situation #4—
You're shopping with your mom at the grocery store. You notice that all candy bars are on sale for 15 percent off. They have your favorite kinds and they're such a good deal. But you know your mom won't buy them and you only have $2, which you were planning to give for the special offering at church.

1. Seeing the hook. (What's the temptation?)

2. Being attracted by the bait. (What causes the attraction?)

3. Possible choices. (What are your choices?)

4. Take action. (Does the action hook you or let you "swim" free?)

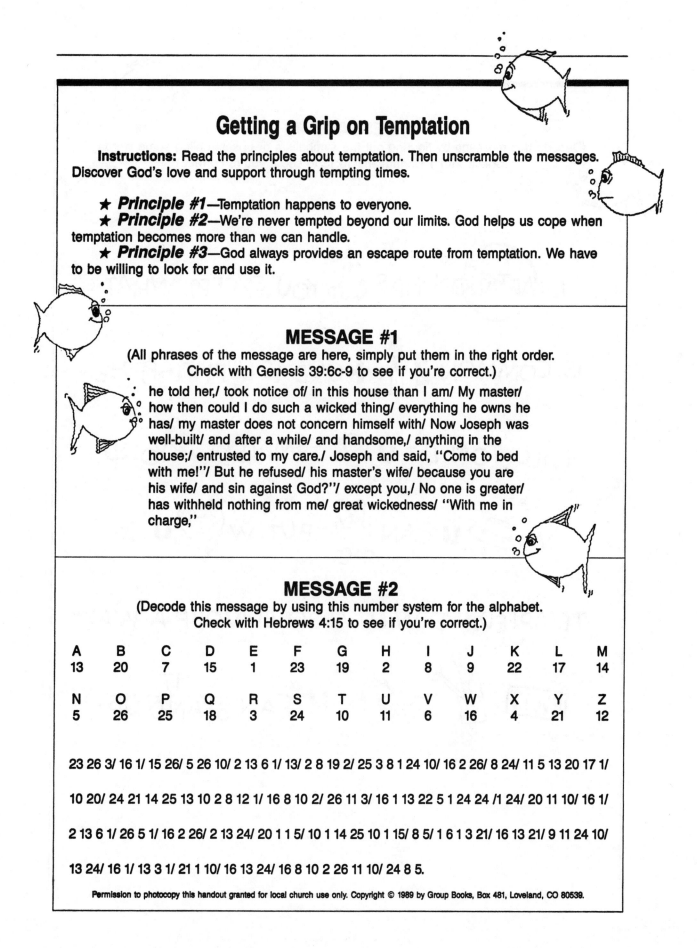

Getting a Grip on Temptation

Instructions: Read the principles about temptation. Then unscramble the messages. Discover God's love and support through tempting times.

★ *Principle #1*—Temptation happens to everyone.
★ *Principle #2*—We're never tempted beyond our limits. God helps us cope when temptation becomes more than we can handle.
★ *Principle #3*—God always provides an escape route from temptation. We have to be willing to look for and use it.

MESSAGE #1
(All phrases of the message are here, simply put them in the right order.
Check with Genesis 39:6c-9 to see if you're correct.)

he told her,/ took notice of/ in this house than I am/ My master/ how then could I do such a wicked thing/ everything he owns he has/ my master does not concern himself with/ Now Joseph was well-built/ and after a while/ and handsome,/ anything in the house;/ entrusted to my care./ Joseph and said, "Come to bed with me!"/ But he refused/ his master's wife/ because you are his wife/ and sin against God?"/ except you,/ No one is greater/ has withheld nothing from me/ great wickedness/ "With me in charge,"

MESSAGE #2
(Decode this message by using this number system for the alphabet.
Check with Hebrews 4:15 to see if you're correct.)

A	B	C	D	E	F	G	H	I	J	K	L	M
13	20	7	15	1	23	19	2	8	9	22	17	14

N	O	P	Q	R	S	T	U	V	W	X	Y	Z
5	26	25	18	3	24	10	11	6	16	4	21	12

23 26 3/ 16 1/ 15 26/ 5 26 10/ 2 13 6 1/ 13/ 2 8 19 2/ 25 3 8 1 24 10/ 16 2 26/ 8 24/ 11 5 13 20 17 1/

10 20/ 24 21 14 25 13 10 2 8 12 1/ 16 8 10 2/ 26 11 3/ 16 1 13 22 5 1 24 24 /1 24/ 20 11 10/ 16 1/

2 13 6 1/ 26 5 1/ 16 2 26/ 2 13 24/ 20 1 1 5/ 10 1 14 25 10 1 15/ 8 5/ 1 6 1 3 21/ 16 13 21/ 9 11 24 10/

13 24/ 16 1/ 13 3 1/ 21 1 10/ 16 13 24/ 16 8 10 2 26 11 10/ 24 8 5.

MESSAGE #3

(Decode this message by figuring out the symbolism or unscrambling some words.
Check with 1 Corinthians 10:13 to see if you're correct.)

TEMPTATION HAS C's'd YOU EXCEPT WHAT

IS COMMON 2 👤. ✝ GOD IS LUFHTIAF; HE

WILL TON LET U 🐝 TEMPTED 🐝 YOND

W-🎩 U CAN 🧸. BUT W-🐓 U R

TEMPTED, HE WILL ALSO EDIVORP A WAY

EXIT 📝 T-🎩 U CAN STAND UP / IT.

By Kathleen Boyd

Feed the Hungry

When we think of hungry and needy people, our minds probably wander to Africa, India or other faraway countries. We rarely think of hunger in our immediate area. This meeting gives young people a chance to become aware of hunger in their neighborhood or town. It lets them examine their feelings toward hunger outreach. You can use this meeting at Thanksgiving or any other time you want to emphasize hunger and thank God for the gifts he freely gives.

Objectives

In this meeting, upper-elementary kids will:
- ★ collect cans of food for the hungry;
- ★ play a relay to help bag the canned goods;
- ★ create two butcher paper banners on hunger;
- ★ examine hunger in their immediate neighborhood or town;
- ★ brainstorm other ideas to help the needy in their community; and
- ★ eat pizza and thank God for the gifts he freely gives.

Preparation

Organize a food drive for your upper-elementary kids one month prior to this meeting. Ask kids to bring as many cans as they can to the meeting. Tell them there'll be a prize for each can they bring. Have them find cans of meat, potatoes, fruit, vegetables, and so on.

Contact a local food bank to get information about the poor or hungry in your area. The food bank or a local shelter will probably have pamphlets you could distribute. Ask them for the best way to deliver the cans of food you collect. Contact your church office for statistics concerning hunger outreach already underway in your area.

Gather newspapers, magazines, glue, scissors, markers, paper, pencils, Bibles, butcher paper, tape and newsprint. You'll also need pizza, salad ingredients, beverages, plates, tableware, napkins and cups for the meal.

Meet in a large area. You'll need a place to play games and to prepare and eat the food. Ask several adult sponsors to help with this meeting.

Ask local grocery stores to donate shopping bags and canned goods.

The Meeting

1 Collect the cans

 Ask one or two kids to be the "checkers" and check in each member's cans. Tell group members they'll receive one pizza slice later for every canned good they brought. Have the children separate all the canned goods into canned meats, fruits, vegetables, and so on.

2 Butcher paper banners

Tape one large sheet of butcher paper to one wall and another large sheet to another wall.

Distribute newspapers, magazines, glue, scissors and Bibles to the entire group. Ask one person to write at the top of one sheet of butcher paper, "I was hungry and you gave me nothing to eat" (Matthew 25:42). Have kids search their materials and write Bible passages on or tape headlines and pictures to this banner that show our lack of compassion toward the hungry.

Ask another person to write on the other sheet, "I was hungry and you gave me something to eat" (Matthew 25:35). Have kids search their materials and write Bible passages on or tape headlines and pictures to this banner that show our abundance and compassion toward the hungry.

After the banners are finished, ask:

★ What pictures and headlines did you find for each banner?

★ Which banner was easier to create? Why?

Read Matthew 25:31-46. Then read the statistics on hunger in your area. Ask:

★ What does Jesus say about feeding the hungry?

★ How many of you knew that hunger was a problem in our area?

★ How do you feel knowing you have plenty to eat when somebody close to you may be hungry?

★ What would Jesus want us to do to help the hungry?

3 Bagger relay

Have the kids form one line. Beginning at the front of the line, have the first kid say, "Feed," the next say, "The," and the third say, "Hungry." Repeat this pattern down the entire line. Divide the group into three teams. All "Feeds" form one team, and so on. Give each team three grocery bags. Say: We're going to have a chance to feed the hungry. Look at all the cans we've collected. They're separated into piles. On "go," one person will run to the other end and place two cans from each of the piles neatly into your shopping bag, and then run back to the line. The next person will do the same, and so on. The first team to *neatly* pack three bags wins. The winners will be the first ones served pizza later. The bags of canned food will be distributed to our local food shelter.

After the relay is finished, place any remaining canned goods in bags. Ask the children to carry the bags to a storage place until they can be delivered to a food shelter.

4 Mealtime assembly line

Say: We've just heard many facts and figures about the needy and hungry in our area. We've begun to do something about that hunger by collecting canned goods. For the next activity, I want you to think about the food you'll eat. Many people are hungry and rarely receive food such as we're going to taste. Be thankful for the fullness you'll experience after you eat. Afterward, we'll think of other ways to help fill the hungry in our area.

Ask parent-helpers to have the pizza ready at the right time and to place the slices on serving trays. Assign kids to set the tables. Make a salad assembly line—one person puts lettuce in bowls, another adds tomatoes, another adds croutons, a couple of kids deliver the salads to the tables.

Ask the kids to sit down. Offer this prayer of thanksgiving: God, thank you for blessing us with good food to keep us healthy. Help us to open our eyes and be aware of the hunger and needs around us. Help us to reach out and help others. Amen.

Have the parent-helpers serve the pizza to the team that finished the bagging relay first. Everyone receives one piece of pizza for each can he or she brought to the meeting. You might want to set a limit based on the pizza you have. Encourage kids to eat until they're full, but not to overeat. If kids forget to bring cans, they can earn pizza by doing extra clean-up duties. Also, allow kids who brought many cans to give pizza to those who didn't. After the meal, have everyone pitch in to clean up.

5 Reaching out to the hungry

Ask kids to focus on their full feeling. Have them imagine never feeling like that. Discuss ways to help make other people aware of the hunger in their area. Then list the ideas on newsprint. For example, organize another food collection; contact the local papers about their efforts or findings; write an article for the church newsletter. Or go beyond feeding the hungry and develop other parts of the passage in Matthew by organizing a clothing drive, visiting a nursing home or a hospital, or sending magazines or books to a prison. Vote for the group members' top six ideas they'd like to organize.

Divide the group into six smaller groups. Give each small group a piece of paper and a pencil, then assign each group one of the top six ideas. Give each group 10 minutes to discuss ways to carry out the idea. For example, a group could be assigned to contact the local paper and tell about their findings. This group could start writing an article using the facts learned in this meeting. The members could plan a time to call a newspaper editor about printing the story.

As a large group, discuss the plans for the six ideas. Make hunger outreach a focus and reality for your group for the next year—plan to do one hunger-outreach activity every two months.

6 Can do

Gather by the "I was hungry and you gave me something to eat" banner. Close with a "can do" prayer to celebrate the cans of food the kids collected. Say a prayer using the list of outreach ideas you created in activity #5. Precede each idea with the word "can." For example: Dear God, keep us focused on hunger and give us strength to know we . . .

. . . *can* organize another food collection;
. . . *can* contact local papers about our efforts;
. . . *can* write an article for our church newsletter; and
. . . *can* schedule regular events to help the hungry in our community. Amen.

By Karen Ceckowski

At Home in My Church

Many young people feel that church is boring. One cause for that feeling may be that they don't understand their church and how it's run. Use this meeting to help young people see the value of their church. Help them grow beyond the belief that church is boring, and challenge them to begin to feel at home within their church.

Objectives

In this meeting, upper-elementary kids will:
- ★ tour their church building;
- ★ participate in mini-devotions during the tour;
- ★ role play greeters and visitors;
- ★ discuss the importance of being friendly to visitors; and
- ★ look at Jesus' example of church and community.

Preparation

Read the meeting. Gather paper, pencils, 3×5 cards and Bibles. Buy a loaf of long French bread, place it in a brown paper bag and leave it by the communion table or altar of your church. Set up refreshments such as doughnuts, cookies or fruit in your church's social center or kitchen.

Explain to your pastor that you want to take your students on a tour of the church. Make sure it's okay to walk about the church and touch things. Be familiar with the meeting so you can explain exactly what you'll be doing during the tour. If you don't know where your church's cornerstone is, ask the pastor. Part of the meeting takes place by the cornerstone.

Vary the meeting according to your church building and your own beliefs.

The Meeting

. . . .

1 A look at the outside

Meet in front of the church. Once everyone is gathered, hand kids each a piece of paper and a pencil. Ask them to pretend they're artists. Give them five minutes to draw a picture of the outside of their church. Don't put any restrictions on their drawings.

Once they're finished, ask them to explain their drawings. Save the drawings for later.

2 The cornerstone

Read aloud Ephesians 2:19-22. Say: Did you know that our church has a cornerstone? This is the first stone that is placed in a building. Jesus used the idea of a cornerstone to help remind us that he's the foundation and center of our church. Let's try to find the cornerstone of our church and see what it looks like.

Allow kids a few minutes to search, then gather around the cornerstone and read the date the church was built. Ask everyone to pick up a rock—if that's permissible—and keep it as a reminder that Jesus is the solid cornerstone of our church, as well as our lives.

Have the kids follow the leader to the foyer (or narthex) for the next activity.

3 A friendly foyer

While in the foyer or narthex, have students gather around you and discuss these questions:

★ Why does our church have this space before we enter the worship area?

★ Have you ever met any of your friends here or stopped to talk to them? If so, how did that make you feel?

★ Why is it important to have greeters at church?

Let a few students role play greeters and the others role play visitors. Let the greeters greet the visitors and direct them into the worship area. While in the worship area, encourage students to act with the same respect and conduct that is expected of them during a church service. Have kids sit in the front rows. Ask:

★ What qualities in a greeter make visitors feel welcome?

★ How can we all make visitors feel welcome?

4 A look at the worship area

Give kids a few minutes to silently look around their church as if this were the first time they had ever entered it. Now have them close their eyes and remember as many things as they can about what they saw. Ask them to keep their eyes closed and describe things they remember about the inside of their church. Have them open their eyes and discuss:

★ What's one item that's most important to you about the church? Why?

★ What are some things we do to worship together?

★ Why are singing and praying with one another important?

★ What do you think Jesus would have done as a boy in church? Read aloud Luke 2:41-49.

5 A worship celebration

Say: Now we're going to plan our own worship celebration. We'll break up into five small groups. One group will lead us in an opening song, one in a prayer, one in reading scripture, one in a brief sermon and one in a collection or offering.

Divide students into five small groups. If you have a small class, double up on the assignments or eliminate one. Allow 10 minutes to plan the worship segments, then hold the worship celebration. Here are some ideas:

★ *Opening Song*—The song-leading group should choose a song everyone knows, such as "Father, We Adore You" from *Songs* (Songs and Creations) or a favorite hymn from the hymnal.

★ *Prayer*—This group could give 3×5 cards to everyone and have each person write a prayer concern. One person could collect the cards and read the concerns, or this group could lead a silent prayer and have everyone pray for his or her own concern.

★ *Scripture*—This group could choose a favorite passage and share it with the sermon group so the two would complement each other. This group could have one person be the narrator with others taking the speaking parts in the passage or they could do a choral reading of the passage. For example, the group members could choose a Psalm. Then they could divide the large group in half. One side could read the odd verses of the Psalm, and the other half could read the even verses.

★ *Sermon*—These group members could write a brief summary of what the passage means to them. They could lead a "discussion sermon" by letting all sermon-group members say what the passage means.

★ *Collection or Offering*—This group could hand out 3×5 cards to everyone and ask kids to write one gift or talent they could offer to the church. For example, a person who sings well could offer to sing a solo; a person who reads well could offer to read a passage; and a friendly person could offer to be a greeter.

6 The communion table

Invite the students to gather around the communion table or altar in a circle. Ask:

★ Why do we have a table or altar in our church?

★ What's it like around your dining room table at home?

★ What do you think it was like around Jesus' dining room table?

Say: Jesus was from a Jewish family. Mealtimes were important to them. It was a time for everyone to pray, talk together and tell special stories. This is important for us today too. Sometimes we become so busy with school, television, computer games and other things that we hurry and eat our dinner and don't take time to pray or talk with our family. Jesus showed us by his example how important it is to dine together.

Read aloud Matthew 15:32-39, then ask why it was important for Jesus to feed the people. Say: Before Jesus died, he gathered his apostles together and had a last meal.

Have students role play the Last Supper. Be sure they take this seriously. Read aloud one of the Passover passages and have the kids act it out as you read (Matthew 26:26-30; Mark 14:22-26; or Luke 22:14-20).

Gather everyone around the table in a circle again and ask them all to hold hands. Say you're going to eat a small meal together. Take out the loaf of bread and break off a piece. Pass the bread and have kids each break off a piece and think about one way they can model Jesus' example around their own table at home. For example, they can be interested in the people around them and ask how their day has been.

Invite kids to discuss ways they can model Jesus' example. Then let everyone eat their bread together. Close with this prayer: God, help us know the importance of Jesus, and the importance of praying and eating together. Help us to feel more at home in our church. Amen.

7 A taste of the snacks

Take the students to the area where your church gathers for coffee and doughnuts or church dinners. As kids are enjoying the snack you prepared beforehand, explain this area's importance for your church. Let them know that it's important for the people to come together for worship and also for fun, recreation and fellowship. This is what being a church community is all about. It's important to be a family and celebrate by spending time with each other.

8 Other ideas

Here are some alternate activities to help your kids feel even more at home with their church:

★ Find out if your church sponsors any food pantries or other places that serve the needy in your community. Take the kids to visit these places and discuss why it's important to reach out to others as Jesus did.

★ Have the kids interview some of the church choir members and find out why singing during worship is special to them.

★ Have people from your church visit your meeting; for example, the president of the congregation, the secretary of the education committee, the custodian, the nursery coordinator. Play "What's My Line?" Let kids ask yes-and-no questions of each person and try to guess what each person does in your church.

★ Make a bulletin board with the drawings of the church from activity #1. Title the bulletin board "Jesus Is Our Cornerstone."

By Terry Vermillion

Who Came to the Manger?

What was that first Christmas really like? Were there donkeys, cattle, sheep, shepherds, wise men and angels? Upper-elementary kids have heard several songs and participated in Christmas programs for years; and they *know* there were all kinds of animals and people who came to see the baby Jesus.

Luke, however, mentions only the flocks and doesn't even say that the shepherds took their sheep to the manger. Luke doesn't even mention the wise men. We find that part of the Christmas story in Matthew 1:18—2:14. This meeting lets kids compare the biblical accounts of Christ's birth to the traditional Christmas program at church.

Objectives

In this meeting, upper-elementary kids will:
★ compare scriptural accounts of the first Christmas with their own thoughts about it;
★ paint a nativity display for the church; and
★ get a fresh perspective on Christ's birth.

Preparation

Read the meeting. Gather all the materials you'll need to paint a nativity scene (tempera paint, brushes, newspaper, tables, chairs, posterboard). You'll also need a Bible, pencils, scissors, animal crackers, masking tape or poster putty, a blackboard and chalk. Each student will need to bring a large old shirt.

On separate slips of paper, write names of animals common in the Holy Land, such as sheep, camel and donkey. These will be used to form small groups, so prepare two to six of each animal—depending on the number of children you choose to have in each group.

Ask parents to help you set up a painting area and a place for the paintings to dry. See "Quick Tips for Handling Paint" for suggestions.

The Meeting

1 Animals at the manger

Hand out the slips with animal names as children arrive. Say: Keep your animal a secret. On "go," act like the animal on your slip and find everyone else who is the same kind of animal. When you find the rest of your kind, sit down with your herd.

2 The manger scene

After groups are formed, give each group one minute to think of animals that might have been at the manger when Jesus was born. When one minute has passed, ask each group to name an animal. List the animals on the blackboard as they're named. Go around the room several times until all ideas have been given.

Read aloud the most familiar account of the Nativity from Luke 2:1-20. Tell the herds to act like their animal when they hear it named during the reading. Since "flocks" are the only animals mentioned, only the sheep should perform. Ask:

★ Were you surprised that only the sheep got a turn? Why or why not?

★ Why do we think that all kinds of animals were at the manger?

★ What other ideas do we have about the time when Jesus was born?

★ How do we display the nativity scene at Christmas? Who's there? Are shepherds there? wise men? angels? donkeys? sheep? cows?

Say: Luke's story tells us about angels, shepherds and sheep. Listen while I read Matthew's story about Jesus' birth. Notice that Matthew tells us about the wise men and the star.

Read aloud Matthew 1:18—2:14.

3 The rest of the scene

Ask the kids to try to remember all the people and animals from the two Bible accounts. List these on the board. Refer to Matthew 1:18—2:14 and Luke 2:1-20 if you need to. Then say: We're going to paint a nativity scene with these people and animals. Each of you can choose what you want to paint.

It doesn't matter if you end up with five sheep and no donkey. It's best to let the kids choose something they feel they can draw.

Give each child a small piece of posterboard and a pencil. Encourage them to think about what makes each animal or person unique: the fluffy white wool on a sheep, the shepherd's crook. Then have them lightly sketch their drawing. Offer positive comments about each person's work, but don't help the kids draw.

When they've finished drawing, let them paint the people and animals. Those who finish early can paint four posterboard strips brown for the stable. It can look like this:

When the kids finish, put the paintings in a safe place to dry. Wash hands and clean up.

4 ✦ Old McDonald's animals
While the paintings are drying, play a fun game. Since not all the groups were called to perform during the scripture reading in activity #1, give them a turn now. Form a circle. Sing "Old McDonald," using the names of the animals in activity #1. As each animal is named, the children belonging to that herd should come to the center of the circle and act like their animal. After each performance lead everyone in an overly enthusiastic round of applause. Change the words to the song to fit the Christmas theme:

Imagine that first Christmas scene,
E-I-E-I-O
And in that scene they had some sheep,
E-I-E-I-O
With a baa baa here, and a baa baa there,
Here a baa, there a baa, everywhere a baa baa,
Imagine that first Christmas scene,
E-I-E-I-O

Quick Tips for Handling Paint

1. Cover everything—Put newspapers on tables and chairs. Have each student bring a large old shirt. Roll up the sleeves and put the shirt on backward. Button the top button. This allows the most coverage for the least effort. After painting, put shirts in a cardboard box without a lid. Shirts will dry and be ready to use the next day. Once or twice a year, run the shirts through a wash-and-dry cycle. To save time don't put names on shirts, simply hand out the top shirt to the first child.

2. Mix thick paint—Mix your own tempera paints to the consistency of mayonnaise. This may cost a bit more, but there are fewer splashes and drips. Mix paints in cups or jars, then pour into wide flat plates to use. The plastic plates that come in gourmet microwave dinners are great for this.

3. Remind the kids that the brush belongs to the paint—Have enough brushes for each child, but explain that the brush belongs to the paint, not to the child. When a child is finished using red and wants to use blue, the red brush must be returned to the red paint and a blue brush picked up. This eliminates messy rinsing and mixing. If your project requires mixing colors, use large dishpans of water for the rinsing. Have a large, damp sponge next to each dishpan for "drying" the brush. As the children finish rinsing they should rub the brush back and forth across the sponge.

4. Find a place for finished projects to dry—Finished projects should be moved as soon as possible to avoid being ruined. Set up a newspaper-covered area away from the paint area. This works well if it can be placed between the painting area and the hand-washing area so children can deposit their work on the way to clean up; then they can view their work on the way back to the group.

5. Clean up fast—Remove paints and brushes as soon as projects are finished. Brushes can be laid flat in a dishpan of water until after the meeting, if needed. Rinse brushes with water, then wash with dishwashing liquid. Shape bristles lightly with fingers. Let brushes dry laying flat, if possible. Many brushes are assembled by gluing the bristles to the handle. If they're dried standing on end, the water draining into the handle may soften the glue and loosen the bristles. When dry, store in a coffee can with handles down. Never leave brushes standing with bristles down, either wet or dry.

5 Christmas animal cookie snack

Munch on animal or Christmas cookies. Sing favorite Christmas songs such as "Away in a Manger" and "Silent Night." Check the paintings to see if they're dry. If they are, distribute scissors and have kids help cut out the shapes. If they aren't dry, set up another time for kids to help cut out the shapes and arrange the nativity scene.

6 Manger arrangers

Let kids help you hang the creation in a prominent place in the church. Posterboard is heavy, so plan on using extra-wide masking tape or a lot of poster putty to attach the artwork to walls. Now, stand back and admire the results.

PART 2:

My Self

By Dr. Scott E. Koenigsaecker

God Loves You—Inside and Out

Upper-elementary children may ask several important questions about their identity:

★ Who am I really?

★ How do others view me?

★ What's my worth?

If kids listen to secular perspectives, they discover that their worth is determined by their ability to produce something, look good or be popular. The Bible is the best source for answering these important questions of life.

This meeting will help students evaluate their self-perceptions in terms of God's Word. As an advertisement stated, "Kids have no trouble learning to look good on the outside, but when it comes to looking good inside, they need your help."

Objectives

In this meeting, upper-elementary kids will:

★ play a game that highlights the difference between "outward" and "inward" personal qualities;

★ identify and list the fruit of the Spirit found in Galatians 5:22-23;

★ decide which fruit of the Spirit each student displays; and

★ affirm each group member's inward personal qualities.

Preparation

Read the meeting. Gather Bibles, pencils, paper, magazines, copies of "The Inside Story" and "You Are So Beautiful to Me" handouts and sticky address labels. You'll need enough labels so each student has one for each group member.

Make four stacks of three to four magazines. Place the four stacks in four different locations in the room.

Find two identical cups. Smear dirt on the outside of one and on the inside of the other. Put them in a bag so no one can see them.

Prepare refreshments. Read activity #5 and choose which option you want for this meeting.

TheMeeting

. . . .

1 Search and find
Randomly assign kids to one of the four stacks of magazines. Open this meeting with a game called "Magazine Scavenger Hunt." Say: I'll read a description of an ad or an item. Your job is to search your stack of magazines for a picture of what I'm describing, rip it out and hold it up. The first team to do this wins five points. We'll do this 10 times. The team with the most points wins.

Use these descriptions and add your own:

★ Find a person who looks like he or she has no cares in the world.

★ Find a person who looks extremely wealthy.

★ Find a person who looks extremely talented.

★ Find a picture of a luxurious dream vacation.

★ Find a picture of a most-desired car.

★ Find a picture of a good-looking man.

★ Find a picture of a good-looking woman.

★ Find a picture of a person who's in great shape.

Follow up this game by saying: If we look at all the pictures that we've torn out, we notice that exterior qualities such as gorgeous hair, good-looking skin and a great body are important. We notice that material possessions such as cars, houses and vacations are desirable. But do exterior qualities really make the person? Do expensive possessions really make a person happy? Can we tell which people in the pictures are nice, helpful, fun or Christian? No, we can't, because qualities like these are inward qualities that don't show up in a picture. Today we'll focus on seeing ourselves as God sees us—from the inside out.

2 The inside story
Gather the kids around you for this object lesson. Take the cups from the bag and hold them up where everyone can see only the outside. Then ask: If you were really thirsty and needed to use one of these cups to get a drink of water, which one would you choose?

Naturally, they'll pick the cup that looks clean on the outside. Then say: I know that most of you have picked this cup that's clean on the outside. But if I turned these cups toward you so that you could see the inside of the cups, then which one would you choose?

Most kids will change their minds and choose the cup that's dirty on the outside and clean on the inside. Then say: You changed your mind, didn't you? This is a good illustration of what God is most concerned with in our life—the inside. As we saw confirmed for us in the opening activity, the media encourage us to focus on our outward appearance—how our hair looks, what clothes we wear, whether our skin is clear or not. But how often do we see an advertisement trying to sell us something to help us look better on the inside? Not often, if ever! God wants us to be clean and good-looking on the inside because that's what really counts. Let's look at some of those inward qualities God would like us to develop.

Ask kids to get in the same groups from activity #1. Give each person a piece of paper and a pencil, and give each group a Bible. Have each group read aloud Galatians 5:22-23. Assign each group a different fruit of the Spirit and have the members make up a magazine advertisement to encourage others to buy it. After about five minutes, let the groups present their ads. (Provide additional craft materials if you want.)

Give each person "The Inside Story" handout and have students evaluate their inward beauty in terms of the fruit of the Spirit. In their small groups, have the students each tell three qualities they feel best about and why, and two qualities they feel need further "beautification" and why.

3 You are so beautiful to me

Give each student a "You Are So Beautiful to Me" handout, and enough address labels so they have one for every person in their small group. Ask students to write their name on their handout. Then have students list on the labels one quality they think is really "beautiful" or great about each person in their group (one quality per person per label). Encourage students to identify the inward, personal qualities that make each person special. Remind them of the inward qualities they just talked about.

Start with the oldest person in the group and have the other members each tell their affirmations to that person, one at a time, by affixing their label to that person's "You Are So Beautiful to Me" handout. Have each student tell why or how this person exhibits this quality. Then move clockwise until each person has been affirmed.

4 Fruit of the Spirit prayer

Start with the person whose birthday is closest to today. In the small groups, have students describe the two fruits of the Spirit they'd most like to have. The person on their left will pray for them. Have students pray for one another. Such a prayer might be as simple as: "Dear God, I want to pray for David today that you'd help him develop more patience and joy. Thank you for David and all he is and does."

5 Fruit-filled refreshments

Here are two options you could try for refreshments:

★ Cover some containers of different kinds of ice cream and different kinds of cookies. On each container place a sign indicating one fruit of the Spirit. Let each person make three selections, choosing fruits of the Spirit he or she wants to show in his or her life.

★ Make a fruit salad. Identify different fruits with the fruit of the Spirit; for example, apples=joy, pears=peace, bananas=patience, and so on. Then give each group a recipe indicating the number of each fruit of the Spirit that should be added to the fruit salad; for example, two joys, one peace, one patience, and so on. Eat the fruit and be thankful!

The Inside Story

Instructions: On a scale of 1 to 10 (1=the fruit that shines brightest in your life; 10=the fruit that needs the most "beautification"), rate the following fruits of the Spirit according to how you display them in your life.

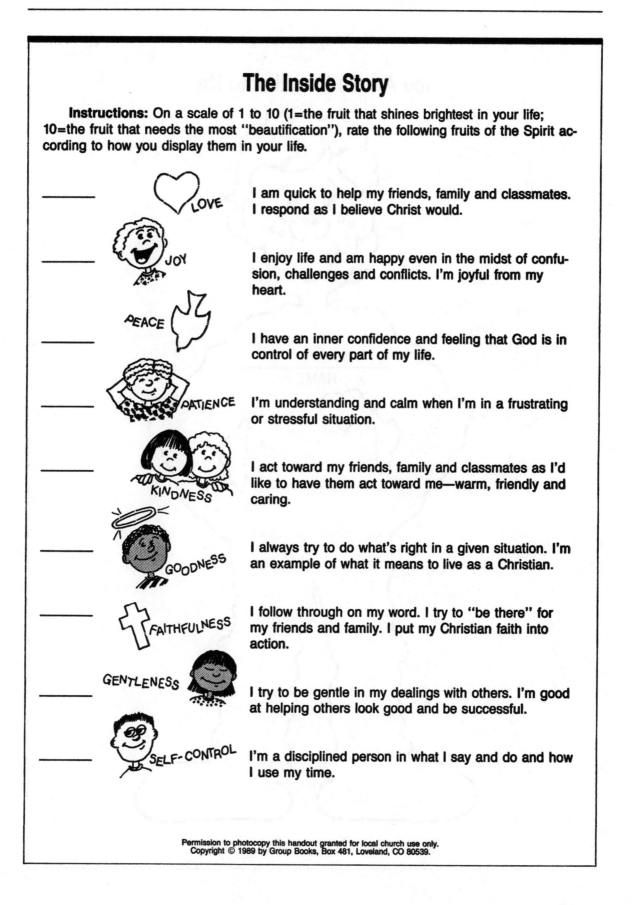

_____ LOVE — I am quick to help my friends, family and classmates. I respond as I believe Christ would.

_____ JOY — I enjoy life and am happy even in the midst of confusion, challenges and conflicts. I'm joyful from my heart.

_____ PEACE — I have an inner confidence and feeling that God is in control of every part of my life.

_____ PATIENCE — I'm understanding and calm when I'm in a frustrating or stressful situation.

_____ KINDNESS — I act toward my friends, family and classmates as I'd like to have them act toward me—warm, friendly and caring.

_____ GOODNESS — I always try to do what's right in a given situation. I'm an example of what it means to live as a Christian.

_____ FAITHFULNESS — I follow through on my word. I try to "be there" for my friends and family. I put my Christian faith into action.

_____ GENTLENESS — I try to be gentle in my dealings with others. I'm good at helping others look good and be successful.

_____ SELF-CONTROL — I'm a disciplined person in what I say and do and how I use my time.

You Are So Beautiful to Me

NAME

By Paul Woods

Values of Gold

"**Y**es, I traded my new book to Joey for his football helmet! What does it matter why?"

Elementary kids don't often think about what makes them do the things they do. But there are things that help us choose how to act in any given situation. They are our values—things that we feel are important in our lives. From the above quote, we can see that reading must have been more of a value for Joey and sports must have been more of a value for the boy who was speaking.

Because upper-elementary kids are still concrete thinkers and the concept of "values" is rather abstract, kids may have a hard time sorting out what values really are. But, since many values that will stick with us for life are formed during the elementary years, it's important to help kids form the right ones now.

Use the concrete learning experiences, the evaluation activities and the discussion questions in this session to help your kids begin that sorting-out process. And at the same time, give them some biblical guidance for forming values that will be pleasing to God.

Objectives
In this meeting, upper-elementary kids will:

★ think about what helps them make the choices they make;

★ discover what things God considers important;

★ demonstrate one of God's values; and

★ choose what they want to make important values in their lives.

Preparation
Read the meeting. Each young person will need a pencil, Bible, scissors, and a copy of the "What Do I Want in Life?" and "One Value Bill" handouts. You will also need a chalkboard and chalk or newsprint and markers. Prepare three large envelopes by writing one of the following titles in big print on each one: "Top Choices," "Important Choices" and "Least Important Choices." Have refreshments ready that are the same as the food items in activity #2.

In the middle of the room, set up a circle of chairs facing outward. Have a record or tape to play for the musical chairs game in activity #1.

Gather a box of prizes. None of the prizes should cost more than a dollar, but be sure the prizes are greatly varied—both in kind and cost. Also be sure that some would be more attractive to girls than boys, and vice versa. Have a few more prizes than you have kids in your group. Here are some suggestions: gumball, pack of gum, wrapped celery stick, wrapped carrot stick, pieces of fruit, inexpensive toys (like party favors), cheap jewelry, candy bar, penny, nickel, dime, quarter, golf tee, rubber ball, pencil, eraser, package of Kool-Aid, can of pop, carton of milk, can or box of juice, can of soup. (If it's impossible to gather prize items, adapt the activity and just use slips of paper with the names of items written on them. However, the effect of the experience will be drastically lessened.)

Cut out 16 "coins" (circles about 1 1/2 inches in diameter) from gold or yellow construction paper. Early arrivers could help you with that task. On one side of each circle write "God's Gold."

Recruit volunteers to help tabulate kids' responses, to help serve refreshments and to lead parts of the meeting.

The Meeting

1. Musical madness

Play musical chairs with your kids. Explain to them that there is one less chair than there are players, and the object of the game is to get seated on a chair when the music stops. Only one person is allowed per chair.

Choose music that your kids would like, and play it on a record or tape player. Each time you stop the music, have the student left without a chair take one chair from the circle and sit off to the side. When you're down to one person, declare that person the winner. Bring the rest of the kids together, and discuss the following questions:

★ What made you act the way you did in that game?

★ Are you usually that selfish in real life? Explain.

★ Why would someone act differently in a game like this than in real life?

2 Pick a prize

Display on a table the prizes you gathered. Say: We had a winner in the musical chairs game, but everyone deserves a prize.

Let the winner go first, and then let kids each choose a prize, going in reverse alphabetical order. Don't let anyone consume the edible or drinkable prizes till later. When everyone has a prize, talk about the prize-choosing experience. Have each student answer the first question, then discuss the others as a group. Encourage kids to give reasons for each answer.

★ Why did you choose the prize you chose?

★ What was important in your choice of a prize: its cost? how much you liked it? hunger? thirst? how much you thought others would like it? how healthy you thought it was?

Say: What you chose shows at least a little bit about what you think is important. In the musical chairs game, getting a chair was what was important to winning the game, so that's what made you act the way you did. In choosing a prize, what was most important to you helped you choose the prize you did. Things that we think are important in helping us make choices in our lives are called values. The values we live by help determine how we act.

3 The big V

Distribute copies of the "What Do I Want in Life?" handout. Have your kids cut apart the 24 different things that some people want in life. Then say: Now look at those 24 possible values and choose which three would be at the top of your list of things you want in life. Without letting anyone else see what you chose, take those three slips and put them in the envelope marked Top Choices.

Have kids line up to put their slips in the envelope so that no one will be crowding around to see what others put in.

When all the kids have put their top three choices in the envelope, have an adult leader start tabulating the slips in the envelope. Also, have each student choose three more slips to put in the next envelope, Important Choices. Explain that these are to be the things they would choose next after their top choices. Follow the same procedure for putting the slips in the envelope.

Finally, have your kids choose three slips to put in the Least Important Choices envelope. Again, use the same procedure.

While adult volunteers complete tabulating the three values most often chosen for each envelope, say: In a survey of 8,000 kids between the fifth and ninth grades, the top choice on this survey was "To have a happy family life." Second was "To get a good job," and third was "To do something important." "To do well in school," "To make my parents proud" and "A world without war" were close behind. The lowest four choices were "To have lots of money," "To be different from other kids," "To do what I want to do" and "To be good in music, drama or art." Now let's take a look at our own choices.

Have your volunteers report the findings from the envelopes. Discuss why kids think those values are or are not important to most of the kids in the group.

4 God's gold

Say: We've seen what values are, and we've discovered what is important to some of us. Now let's look at some values that are important to God.

Divide your group into two teams, and give each team eight "God's Gold" coins. Write the following two references on a chalkboard: Micah 6:8 and Colossians 3:12-14. Have kids read aloud both of these passages in their teams, find eight different things that God values and write one of those things on each of their coins. See which team can complete its eight coins first.

When the first team finishes, go over the values listed on both teams' coins, alternating teams as you go through the coins. For each one, have kids suggest at least one way they can show that value in their lives. Be sure kids save their coins for the closing activity.

5 Sharing the wealth

It's refreshment time. Tell the kids that the ready-to-eat-or-drink items from the prizes are the refreshments for this meeting. Ask who is willing to share their prize with the rest of the group. When kids begin sharing, have the volunteers bring out more of the same items so that everyone gets some. As kids eat, ask: What values are the kids who have shared their food showing?

6 Value to keep

Distribute copies of the "One Value Bill" handout. Have kids look at the values they wrote on their coins earlier. Students each should choose one thing that they really want to make an important value in their life and write it on their "One Value Bill."

Close with prayer, letting kids express to God what they most want to make an important value in their lives. Encourage kids to take home their "One Value Bills" and keep them as reminders of what values they want to exhibit in their lives.

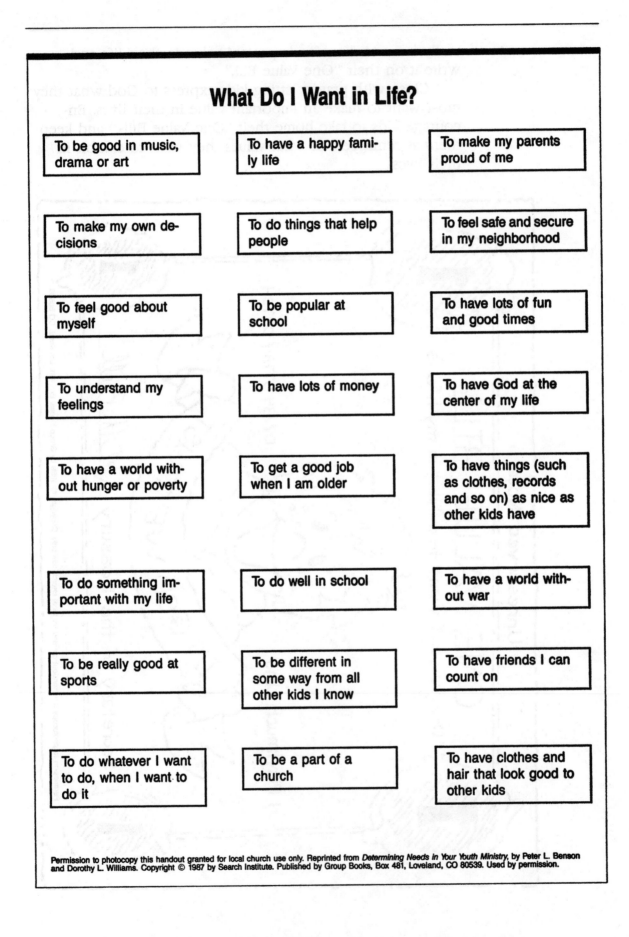

What Do I Want in Life?

To be good in music, drama or art	To have a happy family life	To make my parents proud of me
To make my own decisions	To do things that help people	To feel safe and secure in my neighborhood
To feel good about myself	To be popular at school	To have lots of fun and good times
To understand my feelings	To have lots of money	To have God at the center of my life
To have a world without hunger or poverty	To get a good job when I am older	To have things (such as clothes, records and so on) as nice as other kids have
To do something important with my life	To do well in school	To have a world without war
To be really good at sports	To be different in some way from all other kids I know	To have friends I can count on
To do whatever I want to do, when I want to do it	To be a part of a church	To have clothes and hair that look good to other kids

By Linda Snyder

Commercial Break

For more than 23 hours each week, the average elementary kid is glued to the TV set. During that time, he or she will probably see more than 500 commercials. Everything is advertised. Kids can tell you hundreds of positive reasons to buy a certain product, yet they often can't tell you one positive thing about themselves. Their self-esteem is damaged by those they love, their peers, the media and sometimes even themselves.

Objectives

In this meeting, upper-elementary kids will:

★ participate in a commercial sing-down to experience the selling power of musical tunes in advertising;

★ share their strong points by creating a commercial about themselves;

★ listen to each other's commercials and appreciate individual talents and personalities; and

★ thank God each person is uniquely and wonderfully made.

Preparation

Read the meeting. Gather paper, pencils and several kinds of soft drinks. Gather 15 to 20 items that are advertised often on television, such as Coke, Pepsi, Kraft products, Bic pens and so on. Place them on a table and cover it with a sheet. You'll also need a Bible, scissors, markers and a large piece of cloth. If you have a large group, you will need to cut out several gingerbread-people shapes from the cloth ahead of time.

Videotape or record on audio tape about two to three minutes of commercials. Kids will be preparing their own commercials during this meeting. You may want to record their completed commercials on videotape or cassette tape. If so, bring the necessary equipment.

The Meeting

1 Getting to know you

Direct kids to the table where you've set out several kinds of soft drinks. Have them pick their favorite drink and start sipping. While kids sip their favorite drinks, have them mingle. They have five minutes to talk to as many people as they can. They have to exchange two facts: their name and why their drink is their favorite.

2 Memory game

Gather the kids by the table of 15 to 20 items you have covered. Tell the kids that you'll take the sheet off and pick up the items one at a time. They must try to remember everything that's on the table. After you have done so, cover the items again.

Distribute paper and pencils. Tell the kids to write down all the items they can remember. After about three to five minutes, see who remembered the most. Award a can of his or her favorite soft drink to the winner.

3 Commercial sing-down

Say: You might have remembered more of the items if we had made up a song to advertise them and cement them in your memory. Music really helps us remember things. Listen to some of today's commercials that help us remember certain products.

Play the tape of TV commercials.

Divide the group into two teams (guys versus girls or January through June birthdays versus July through December birthdays). Give each team five minutes to remember and write down commercials that have musical lines in them. The more they think of, the better chance they have of winning. The team will need to sing aloud each commercial phrase.

Call time and bring the two teams back together. Have them sit in two separate circles. Take turns asking each team to stand and sing one of its commercial tunes. Alternate until one team has run out of tunes. Be sure that someone on each team keeps track of what both teams have sung. If a tune is repeated, that team loses. You may have more than one song for the same product; for example, Coke commercials vary their tunes. The teams earn points as they remem-

COMMERCIAL BREAK ★ 65

ber different tunes. The last team to sing a commercial tune wins.

When the game is over and one team has been declared a winner, ask:

★ Were you surprised at the number of tunes you knew? Why or why not?

★ Since commercials are made to sell things, what were some of the good selling points about the commercials you sang?

4 Group commercial

Say: Since music helps us remember things, let's create a musical, group commercial to help us remember how wonderful our group is. Let's think of all the things that make us special and put the words to the tune "Jesus Loves Me."

An example of a musical, group commercial is: "We are special, yes we are. We can sing and play guitar. We can read and write and pray. God made us a special way. Yes, we are special. Yes, we are special. Yes, we are special. God made us just like him."

Take about 10 minutes for this activity.

5 Marvelous me commercials

Say: We sang all about the great products on TV commercials. We also created a musical commercial about our fantastic group. We, as individuals, certainly have great qualities. Maybe you have a great smile or gorgeous eyes. Maybe you're really smart or a good friend. Find a partner. Help each other write all kinds of good things about yourselves. Use your lists to create a commercial that sells your partner, because he or she is special. You can make your commercial to a tune, or you can just say it. For example: Judy: bright, witty, intelligent, caring. You need her for a friend.

Distribute paper and give pairs each several minutes to create their two commercials. You can share these commercials in one of three ways. Choose the one for your group:

★ Take turns having the pairs introduce each other to the group by singing or saying their commercials.

★ Videotape the commercials privately. Show the videotape to the entire group.

★ Record the commercials on audio tape privately. Play the tape and let all group members listen.

6 The magic cloth

Dramatically unfurl your piece of fabric. Tell the kids to imagine that this is the material God used to form people when he created the world. Describe how wonderful the material is.

Begin cutting gingerbread-people shapes out of the material. As you cut, explain that part of the magic of the material is that no two pieces are ever alike. Some will have blue eyes; some will be short; some will be skinny; some will be strong; some will love school; some will love sports.

Continue cutting and talk about how things in our lives may affect us. Some people experience warm, loving families; others experience sadness and brokenness. Say: Each one of us is unique. We are all different in some way. Some of the differences can be seen in the way we look. Some of the differences are in our hearts. But everyone was made by God with his special magic cloth. Since the cloth God used to make us is wonderful and good, each one of us must be wonderful and good. In the Bible, King David talks to God. Listen as he thanks God for making him wonderful and good. Read aloud Psalm 139:13-14.

Distribute a gingerbread shape and marker to each person. Then have the kids write "I am fearfully and wonderfully made" on one side. On the other side, have them write one positive quality about themselves they want to thank God for.

Close with a silent prayer while kids hold their gingerbread shapes. Ask kids to thank God for making them the way he did.

Be sure the kids take home their cloth people to remind them that they're wonderful and good—great commercials of God's love.

By Jim Reeves

"P.L.U.S.": A Problem-Solving Plan

Kids are called on more and more these days to solve problems on their own. Many parents work at full-time jobs and kids come home to empty houses. Some kids don't have the ability to solve problems on their own. This meeting is designed to teach kids an easy way to solve problems. They'll enjoy this time together and learn something at the same time.

Objectives

In this meeting, upper-elementary kids will:

★ learn "P.L.U.S.," an easy plan to systematically solve problems;

★ use their own thoughts and friends' opinions when searching for solutions to problems; and

★ make a mobile to remind them of the problem-solving plan.

Preparation

Read the meeting. Gather copies of "The P.L.U.S. in the Bible" handout, pencils and Bibles. Bring a game that requires a lot of decision-making, such as "Clue."

For each person, place the following in a small sack: one coat hanger, four pieces of yarn, four small pieces of cardboard, scissors, glue, markers, and red, orange, black and yellow construction paper.

Prepare a sample mobile. Make a cardboard symbol of each of the following steps for the "P.L.U.S." problem-solving plan:

P—Cut out a cardboard cloud shape and cover it with black construction paper. This symbolizes "Problems."

L—Cut out a cardboard light bulb shape and cover it with yellow construction paper. This symbolizes "Lots of ideas and choices."

U—Cut out a cardboard heart shape and cover it with red construction paper. This symbolizes "Using your friends, family and other resources."

S—Cut out a cardboard star shape and cover it with orange construction paper. This symbolizes "Successful solution."

Attach each symbol to the coat hanger with a piece of yarn.

The Meeting

 1 Teamwork Divide the group into four equal teams. Place each team in each of the four corners of the room. Say: In this meeting we're going to learn an easy plan to help solve problems. It's called the "P.L.U.S." plan. "P" stands for problems; "L" stands for lots of ideas and choices; "U" stands for using friends, family and other resources; "S" stands for successful solution. We'll learn more about the problem-solving plan later. But first we're going to practice problem-solving by playing a game.

Place a board game in the middle of the room. Describe the game to the four groups as it's described in the rules, only where it says "player," you substitute "team." Play the game as if you have four players, only you have four teams instead. Each team picks a game piece to represent its players during the game. Start the game by having each team choose one member to come to the game board and roll the dice. (For extra fun you could make a large pair of dice out of a couple of boxes.) The team with the largest number rolled on the dice goes first.

The game is played according to the rules. Each team should rotate members so everyone has a turn to roll the dice and move their game piece. The practice in problem-solving comes during the game. Whenever a decision needs to be made, team members must decide together—each person has a say.

Encourage speed and set a time limit of 20 minutes. After the time is up, ask:

★ How did you make decisions along the way?

★ Was it hard to play as a team? Why or why not?

★ What did you learn about making decisions and solving problems during the game?

 2 What would you do if? Gather the kids in a semicircle facing the front. Say: We're going to learn more about solving problems by doing some "What Would You Do If?" role playing. I'll tell a volunteer a situation. The volunteer will think what he or she would do if he or she were faced with that situation and respond accordingly. Do I have a volunteer to go first?

Bring this person up front and describe the situation: You're waiting after school for your friends who are inside taking care of last-minute items for an upcoming school project. You don't want to go home alone. As you wait for them, someone approaches you from across the street. He says: "Hi, my name is John, and I live across the street. I saw you standing here. Can I ask you a favor? I need someone to come over to my house to help me with some stuff in my garage. I need to put this stuff into my car to carry it to a friend's house. I'll be glad to pay you."

Let the young person tell how he or she would respond if this happened. Stop the action after a minute or so. Ask the rest of the group members other ways to solve the problem.

Ask for four volunteers to do another role play. Say: You're all walking down the street carrying skateboards. You're going to a friend's house to play. Suddenly, a big high school kid comes up to you and takes away one of your skateboards. He says: "Hey, kid, this looks just like the skateboard I lost last week at the park. Where did you find it? It's mine, you know."

Let the kids role play what they'd do if they were faced with a similar situation. Stop the action after a minute or so. Ask the rest of the group members other ways they'd solve this problem.

3 "P.L.U.S."

Say: As I said earlier in the meeting, we're going to learn a plan for solving problems called "P.L.U.S."

Repeat what "P.L.U.S" stands for:
★ Problems;
★ Lots of ideas and choices;
★ Using your friends, family and other resources; and
★ Successful solution.

Get back into the four teams. Distribute "The 'P.L.U.S' in the Bible" handouts, pencils and Bibles to each group. Assign each group one of the two Bible stories and have the members circle it on their handout. Tell them they have 15 minutes to read the story and discover how "P.L.U.S." worked for their Bible characters. After groups finish, ask each group to report its findings.

Here's an example of "P.L.U.S" working for Paul and Silas: Their problem was that they were thrown in prison. They had lots of ideas and choices to solve their problem. They could pray, they could sing hymns, they could rely on God. They used these resources God provided, and he solved their problem. God sent an earthquake that opened the prison doors. Added to all that excitement, the jailer became a believer and so did his entire family. What a successful solution to a problem!

4 The "P.L.U.S." project

Say: Each one of us is going to make a mobile that symbolizes what we just learned. Stay in your four teams. Choose one person to come to me and pick up the materials for all of you. This person will come back to your group and hand each of you a bag of material. We're going to make a mobile that looks like this sample. (Show the sample mobile you made.) If you get done early, help someone else.

5 The "P.L.U.S." in our lives

Ask everyone to look at his or her mobile as a reminder of the easy-to-use, problem-solving plan. Then have the kids think of a current problem they're facing. Ask kids each to find one person who's sitting

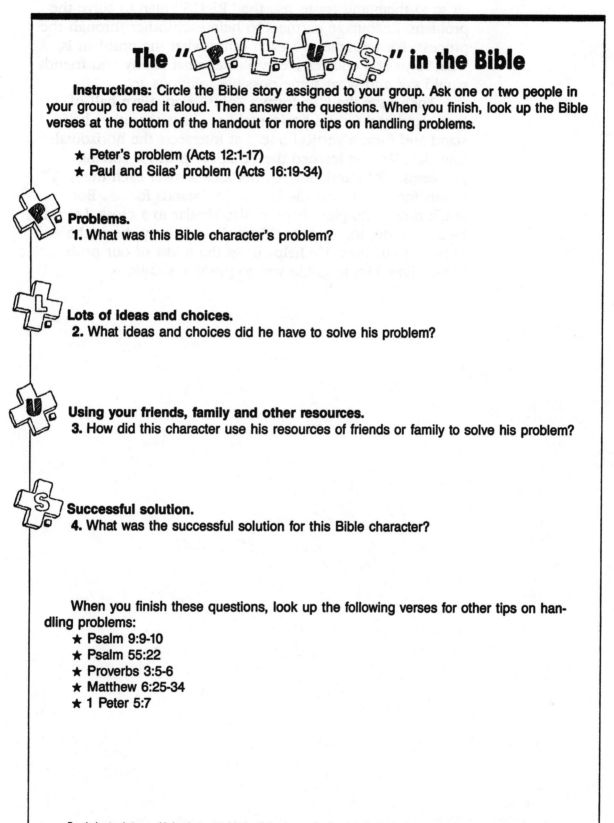

The "P.L.U.S." in the Bible

Instructions: Circle the Bible story assigned to your group. Ask one or two people in your group to read it aloud. Then answer the questions. When you finish, look up the Bible verses at the bottom of the handout for more tips on handling problems.

★ Peter's problem (Acts 12:1-17)
★ Paul and Silas' problem (Acts 16:19-34)

Problems.
1. What was this Bible character's problem?

Lots of ideas and choices.
2. What ideas and choices did he have to solve his problem?

Using your friends, family and other resources.
3. How did this character use his resources of friends or family to solve his problem?

Successful solution.
4. What was the successful solution for this Bible character?

When you finish these questions, look up the following verses for other tips on handling problems:
★ Psalm 9:9-10
★ Psalm 55:22
★ Proverbs 3:5-6
★ Matthew 6:25-34
★ 1 Peter 5:7

close to them and try to use the "P.L.U.S" plan to solve the problem. Encourage partners to help each other through the process. For example, ask each other what the problem is, what ideas and choices are available, what family and friends would say, and what some possible solutions are.

Then have the kids form a "plus" sign. Have half of the kids stand and form a horizontal line; have the other half stand and form a vertical line that intersects the horizontal one. Say: We just learned the "P.L.U.S." plan for solving problems. "P" stands for . . . (let kids answer each time) "L" stands for . . . "U" stands for . . . "S" stands for . . . But you'll notice the plus shape is also similar to a cross. Let this be a reminder to you that Christ should always be at the center of our lives. He helps us in the midst of our problems. Allow him to guide you to positive solutions.

By Dr. Scott E. Koenigsaecker

Tough Decisions

The average person makes hundreds of decisions daily. Sometimes knowing what God wants us to do is easy because we can find answers in the Bible. But sometimes knowing what God wants us to do is difficult because the Bible doesn't directly address some decisions.

God has given us resources to help make tough decisions. He gives us the Bible, prayer, circumstances in our lives, and other Christians. Use this meeting to help students become better equipped to make the tough decisions in their lives.

Objectives

In this meeting, upper-elementary kids will:

★ play a game that helps them experience the difficulty of making decisions;

★ list and discuss why some decisions are easy to make while others are more difficult;

★ evaluate different influences that affect their decisions about drinking alcohol, gossiping, choosing friends, cheating, and obeying parents; and

★ identify and discuss different resources God has given them to handle tough decisions.

Preparation

Read the meeting. Gather 3×5 cards, pencils, copies of "Finding Our Way" and "Who Says What?" handouts, Bibles with concordances, chalkboard and chalk, and special materials for the activities. You'll need several kinds of refreshments, such as popcorn and pop, cheese and crackers, and doughnuts and milk. Kids will have to make a decision about which refreshment they want to eat.

Activity #1 is a version of the game show *Let's Make a Deal*. Contestants make decisions about whether or not to trade an item for another item. Decide how many contestants you want to participate and how many options you want them to choose. You can be the game-show host and wear a suit and carry a microphone. (Ham it up!) You'll need three pencils; three same-size sacks labeled #1, #2 and #3; three same-size boxes labeled #1, #2 and #3. In Sack #1, place a cotton ball; in Sack #2, place a candy bar; in Sack #3, place a pack of gum. In Box #1, place two candy bars; in Box #2, place two packs of gum; in Box #3, place nothing. If you want more than two trades, you will need to prepare more sacks and boxes.

Activity #4 requires some road signs posted in four different locations. Place a Bible by each road sign. Place Road Sign #1 under a bookshelf in the library; place Road Sign #2 in the kitchen; place Road Sign #3 under a trash can; place Road Sign #4 under a Sunday school table. Make each sign a different shape, such as a square, circle, triangle and octagon. Write the following on the signs:

★ *Road Sign #1: The Bible*—We need to read and study the Bible. God helps us make decisions (Psalm 119:105; Romans 8:28-29; 2 Timothy 3:16-17).

★ *Road Sign #2: Prayer*—In prayer, we ask the Spirit to guide us when we make decisions (1 Corinthians 2:9-16; Philippians 4:6-7).

★ *Road Sign #3: Circumstances*—God can direct our lives through the opening of the doors or opportunities of life. We need to be honest about who we are and let God use us, no matter what. (Acts 16:6-10; 17:13-15; Romans 12:2).

★ *Road Sign #4: Other Christians*—Other committed Christians are a valuable resource we often overlook. As members of Christ's body, we need to take advantage of others' insights and understanding (Proverbs 12:15; Ecclesiastes 4:9-10; Colossians 1:9; 4:12).

The Meeting

 1 Let's make a decision Play your own version of the game show *Let's Make a Deal*. The object of the game is to let students make decisions about trading merchandise. Choose three people to be the contestants. Give each one a pencil and say: Hello, contestants. Welcome to *Let's Make a Decision*. You've each been given a pencil for participating in the show. I'll show you three sacks filled with surprises. You'll be able to decide if you want to trade your pencil for one of the sacks. If you trade, you lose the pencil but gain whatever is in the sack—which could be good or bad. If you decide not to trade, you keep your pencil and go back to your seat.

Show the three sacks and let each contestant decide whether or not he or she wants to trade the pencil for one of them. Encourage the other group members to shout encouragement and suggestions to the contestants.

If they decide to trade, take away their pencils and give them their chosen sacks. Now say: Contestants, you've one more chance to decide to trade. You may trade for one of these three boxes. It's your choice. You may also decide to keep your sack (or pencil). If so, you can take your seat.

Let the contestants decide to trade or keep what they already have. Show the end results.

Play this game as many times as you want. If you have more contestants, make more prizes and vary the contents of the containers. After the game, discuss these questions:

★ How did the contestants make their decisions? Was it difficult or easy to decide? Why or why not?

★ How much did other group members' comments affect the decisions?

2 Top tough decisions
Say: With this next activity, we're going to continue discussing decisions we face.

Divide your group into three smaller groups by having kids count off, saying, "Top," "Tough" or "Decisions." All the "Tops" form one group, and so on. Ask each group to think of the top five to 10 toughest decisions they face. Distribute 3×5 cards and pencils to each group and have the members write each tough decision on a separate 3×5 card.

Collect the cards. Say: I'm going to read each tough decision. We're going to score how tough we think each decision is. If you think the decision I read is not-so-tough, hold up one finger; if you think it's pretty tough, hold up five fingers; if you think it's terribly tough, hold up 10 fingers.

Read the decisions and discuss the scores.

3 Who says what?
Have kids stay in the same groups, and distribute the "Who Says What?" handouts and Bibles with concordances. Assign each group one or two of the decisions listed on the handout: drinking, drugs, gossiping, cheating, obeying parents or choosing friends. Have each

group fill in the sheet for its assigned decision. For the section titled "What God Says," encourage students to look up the passages listed under their assigned topic. If time permits, have them use the concordances to look up more passages. Show the kids how to use a concordance; many of them might not be familiar with it.

After the handouts are completed, discuss the insights. Ask:

★ Is there a difference between what God says and what the media, peers and some friends might say?

4 Finding our way

Ask kids to stay in their small groups. Have them line up one behind the other and place their hands on the shoulders of the person in front of them. Each small group is a "car" and the members' job is to "drive" around the area searching for road signs that'll direct them to God's will. Give each car a "Finding Our Way" road map. As each car finds the signs, the passengers should look up each of the scripture passages listed.

After the cars have found all the road signs, have the passengers park and evaluate how well they use the road signs of the Bible, seeking God's direction in prayer, evaluating their circumstances and asking the advice of other committed Christians when they have to make tough decisions.

Say: We're going to see how well you use each road sign when you have to make a tough decision. If you don't use it, move about 10 mph in a slow jogging-in-place motion. If you use it a lot, move about 65 mph by running in place fast.

Read each of the road signs and have the passengers show how much they use them to guide their decisions. Ask:

★ Why is it sometimes hard to pray? read the Bible? listen to others? accept our circumstances?

★ How can we use what we've learned in this meeting to make future tough decisions?

If time allows, take one tough decision and work through it as a large group, using all four road signs.

5 Decisions

Choose one or more of the following activities:

★ Write the word "Decision" vertically on the left side of a chalkboard. Ask students to think of sentences that begin with each letter of the word "Decision" that relate to what they've learned during the meeting. For example:

Depend on God.
Expect the best.
Choose good friends and listen to them.
Insist on prayer.
Seek God's help.
Invite parents to help.
Only trust God.
Never give up.

★ Give each small group a different object, such as a watch, calculator, cup or ruler. Have the members make up a short commercial message that uses their object and makes a point about doing God's will. For example, a group with a rolling pin could say, "Doing God's will helps roll out the lumps and bumps of tough decisions."

★ During a prayer, let students ask God to strengthen them in the areas where they are weak.

 **6 What to eat?** Give kids the choice of several fantastic desserts—but they can only have one! (Set up additional road signs that lead to the goodies!)

Finding Our Way

Instructions: Use these clues as a map to show you the way to the road signs!

★ Road Sign #1: For this sign you will look and look. You'll find it by a place where you'd find a book.

★ Road Sign #2: Looking for this sign is an incredible feat. Search for it in a place where you eat.

★ Road Sign #3: You make incredibly good passengers, I must say. Look for this sign where you throw things away.

★ Road Sign #4: The surface is flat and used all the time, look near the chairs for this very next sign.

Who Says What?

Instructions: Circle your assigned decision, then answer the first three questions below the decisions. Discover the answer to question #4 (what God says) by looking up the scripture passages underneath your assigned decision.

Decisions

Should you drink alcohol?
Proverbs 20:1; 23:20-21, 29-35
Romans 13:11-14
Ephesians 5:18
1 Thessalonians 5:7-9

Should you use drugs?
1 Corinthians 6:19-20
Ephesians 5:15-18
2 Timothy 1:7

Should you obey your parents?
Ephesians 6:1-3
Colossians 3:20
Proverbs 13:1

Should you gossip?
Proverbs 20:19
Romans 1:29-31
Ephesians 4:25-27
1 Timothy 5:13

How should you choose your friends?
Psalm 26:4
Proverbs 12:26
1 Peter 1:22

Should you cheat?
Proverbs 13:6
Luke 16:1-9
Ephesians 4:22-25

Questions

1. What does the media (television, magazines, the movies) say?

2. What do your friends say?

3. What do your parents say?

4. What does God say?

Meeting 13

Questions About Sexuality

Sex is not a topic that's restricted to only teenagers and adults. Elementary kids have questions and they want answers. In this meeting, upper-elementary students will have a chance to ask questions, discuss confusing issues, find God's guidelines, think about right and wrong, and hear about God's promise of forgiveness.

Objectives

In this meeting, upper-elementary kids will:
★ write questions they have about sexuality;
★ search the scripture for God's guidelines;
★ apply the guidelines to confusing issues; and
★ thank God for his never-ending forgiveness and help through stormy times.

Preparation

Before you use this meeting, explain to your kids' parents what you want to do. You might even want to discuss with them what you and they think are the kids' biggest needs in this area. Also, be sure your kids are familiar with basic facts about sexuality. Some kids have learned the basic facts in school or at home, but not all have. It's important for kids to have a foundation of facts; then you can use this meeting for values clarification and scripture searching for God's guidelines on sexuality. Some helpful resources:

Givers, Takers, and Other Kinds of Lovers by Josh McDowell and Paul Lewis (Tyndale House Publishers).

Sex, Dating and Love: Seventy-Seven Questions Most Often Asked by Ray E. Short (Augsburg Press).

Talking With Your Child About Sex: Questions and Answers for Children From Birth to Puberty by Mary S. Calderone and James W. Ramey (Ballantine Books, Inc.).

Read the meeting. Gather 3×5 cards, pencils, Bibles, a washtub of water, animal crackers, 7-Up, a toy boat to use as an "ark" (may find this in the church's nursery), construction paper, yarn, and various colors of bubblegum (one piece for each person). For every pair, you will also need glue, half a walnut shell, toothpick and paper flag.

Follow the example given and make ark-shape name tag necklaces out of construction paper and yarn, one for each person. Write each animal name you choose on two name tags. You'll have two bears, two dogs, two cats, and so on.

Prepare four rooms as needed.

The Meeting

1 Animal patrol

Give each kid a name tag necklace. Have them each write their name on it, flip it over and put it on so others can't see their animal name. Allow a few minutes for kids to pantomime their animal and try to find the other person with the same animal. When they each find their partner, ask them to flip over their name tag necklaces and complete these sentences with their partner:

★ The time I felt most like a (animal on their name tag necklace) was . . .

★ I think this meeting is going to be about . . .

Say: This meeting isn't going to be about animals, pets or the zoo. It's going to be about you. You and sexuality. When God told Noah to build an ark and bring on the animals two by two, male and female, he did it for a reason. He wanted his creation to keep on "being." He wanted them to "be fruitful and multiply."

That's one reason for sex. To reproduce. People have other reasons for sex. Some are good, some are not so good. Today we're going to talk about sexuality and see what God wants us to do. We're going to follow each other two by two to four different rooms. We'll discuss our questions about sexuality, God's guidelines for our questions, the trying times when we're not sure what's right and wrong and God's promise of forgiveness.

Start singing "Rise and Shine," the song about Noah and

the flood from *Songs* (Songs and Creations) and have kids line up two by two with their animal-name partners. Lead the way to the first room.

 2 Questions, questions Have the kids stay with their partners and find a spot in the room that's comfortable. Say: When God spoke to Noah and told him his plans, I'm sure Noah had a lot of questions. It's okay to have questions and ask God for guidance. We might have a lot of questions today concerning sexuality such as "How far is too far?" "How do I know what is right with a person I really like?" We're going to take time now to write down any questions you might have. I'll distribute 3×5 cards and pencils. Write any questions you have about sexuality, one question per card. I'll give you five minutes. When I call time, I'll collect the cards in the "ark." We'll use the questions in the rest of the meeting.

Let the kids write their questions; then collect them in the toy boat. You'll want to sort out any questions that you deem inappropriate. Choose two or three questions and discuss them as a large group. See what kinds of answers and insights the kids have at the beginning of the meeting. Then say: We've tried our best to answer some of these questions now. Let's proceed to the next room to find some guidelines that God can give us.

Sing "Rise and Shine" and have kids line up two by two. Have them follow the leader to the next room.

 3 God's guidelines Let the pairs find a comfortable place in the room. Then say: Just as God gave Noah guidelines for building the ark, God gives us guidelines about sexuality.

As a large group, read the following scripture passages:
★ Matthew 5:27-28; 19:18
★ 1 Corinthians 6:16-17; 7:1-7
★ Ephesians 5:3
★ 1 Thessalonians 4:3-8
★ Hebrews 13:4
After each passage ask:
★ What guideline is God giving us?
Let the pairs discuss their insights. For example, a guideline for Matthew 5:27-28 could be "Think only good thoughts. Bad thoughts can lead to bad behavior."
Give each pair half a walnut shell, a toothpick, paper

flag and glue. Have the pairs build an ark out of the materials. Then on the paper flag, have pairs each write one guideline they think is the most important. Ask the pairs to take their walnut ark with them to the next room.

Sing "Rise and Shine," line up, and progress to the next room.

4. Rainy days and rainy nights

Gather the pairs around the tub of water that has been placed in the center of the room. Say: In Noah's time, Noah did as God asked. He followed God's guidelines, built an ark, gathered the animals, then rode out the storm. Let's find some of the guidelines you thought were most important that can help us through stormy questions with sexuality.

Have pairs share their guidelines. After each pair shares, have that pair float its walnut ark in the water.

Read a few more of the 3×5 card questions. Ask the kids to try to answer these questions using some of the guidelines they found in the scripture.

Say: Now that we've discussed several God-given guidelines, we're going to voice our opinions on whether certain situations are wrong. To do this, we're going to make rain. Here's how:

I'll say a situation. If you think it's questionable, simply snap your fingers. If you think it's pretty bad, clap your hands. If you think it's horrible, stomp your feet. If you think absolutely nothing's wrong with it, give a thumbs-up signal. We can see and hear which situations you think are bad by the amount of rain you make.

Then use these situations:

★ Having sex before marriage
★ Having sex if you love each other but aren't married
★ Having sex but using birth control
★ (Add several other situations from the 3×5 card questions.)

Discuss the rain-making situations as a large group.

★ What were some of the opinions?
★ How do we know what's right and what's wrong?

★ How do God's guidelines help us make these decisions?

Sing "Rise and Shine," line up two by two and proceed to the next room.

5 Promises, promises

Say: At the end of Noah's rainy, stormy experience, God set a rainbow in the sky and promised his long-lasting forgiveness. We're going to pray silently and focus on God's love. God loves us no matter what. He's always there to help us through the gray, stormy times when we don't know what's right or wrong.

Close the silent prayer with a simple "Amen."

Give each person a different color piece of bubblegum. Have the kids chew the bubblegum until it's soft enough to blow a bubble. On the count of three, have kids blow a bubble. Look at the rainbow of colors and think about the promise of God's forgiveness! Then let the kids pop their bubbles and shout, "Thanks for loving me, God!"

6 Feed the ark relay

Top off the season with a rowdy activity called "Feed the Ark Relay" from *Quick Crowdbreakers and Games for Youth Groups* published by Group Books. Divide group into two teams. Split the pairs according to their name tag necklaces, with one animal of each pair in each line. Choose one person in each line to go to the far end of the room and be the "ark" for his or her team. Give one animal cracker to each person in each team. The object of the relay is to "feed the ark." On "Noah," one at a time, each person runs up to the ark, feeds the animal cracker, runs back, and tags the next person—who repeats the process. The first ark full of animals (chewed up and swallowed) wins.

7 Refreshment time

For refreshments, serve animal crackers and sparkling rain water (7-Up).

By Cindy Hansen

Drug Dangers

Why include an upper-elementary meeting about drugs? Upper-elementary kids don't even have the slightest idea or concern about drugs. They're too young. Right? Wrong.

According to research reported in *The Quicksilver Years: the Hopes and Fears of Early Adolescence* by Peter Benson, Dorothy Williams and Arthur Johnson, 40 percent of fifth-graders and 38 percent of sixth-graders surveyed reported worrying quite a bit or very much about drugs and drinking. That percentage grows as kids grow older. According to research reported in *The Youth Ministry Resource Book*, 54 percent of teenagers surveyed say drug abuse among their peers is their top concern.

This meeting helps kids learn to deal with the problem of drug abuse. Kids will learn more about drugs and how to say no without losing their friends. The ideas are adapted from *Drugs, God & Me* by Kathleen Hamilton Eschner and Nancy G. Nelson. Here are some resources to help teach young people more about this topic:

Drugs, God & Me by Kathleen Hamilton Eschner and Nancy G. Nelson (Group Books).

Kids, Drugs and Alcohol: A Parent's Guide to Prevention and Intervention by Anne Harrity and Ann Cristensen (Betterway Publications).

Not My Kid: A Parent's Guide to Kids and Drugs by Beth Polson and Miller Newton (Arbor House Publishers).

Check your telephone directory or a directory of a large city, for these and other self-help groups: Alcoholics Anonymous, Al-Anon, Alateen, Narcotics Anonymous, Adult Children of Alcoholics.

Objectives

In this meeting, upper-elementary kids will:

★ play a game to introduce them to the topic;

★ complete a crossword puzzle to test their knowledge of drugs;

★ brainstorm reasons people may take drugs and think of alternatives to using drugs;

★ role play how they'd react in various "tempting" situations; and

★ complete a Bible study and discover some of God's guidelines concerning this topic.

Preparation
Read the meeting. Gather Bibles, pencils, photocopies of the "Test Your Knowledge About Drugs," "What Does the Bible Say?" and "Situation Simulation" handouts, a blackboard and chalk.

The Meeting

 **1 Overdoser** Gather kids for a quick crowdbreaker to introduce the topic. Have participants stand in a circle in the center of the room. Say: After I give these instructions, I'll ask you to close your eyes while I walk around the circle. I'll secretly touch someone on the back, and that person will be the "Overdoser." The Overdoser's goal is to kill all the group members by winking at them one at a time before anyone discovers who he or she is. Only the Overdoser can wink at people.

When the game begins, people should open their eyes and mingle around the room, looking other people in the eye. Approximately every 30 seconds, the Overdoser should wink at a person to give him or her an overdose. When you're winked at, you must wait 10 seconds, then die by falling to the floor. Victims can be melodramatic if they want but should not try to reveal the Overdoser's identity.

The object of this game is to try to identify the Overdoser before you become a victim. As soon as you think you can identify the Overdoser, stand still and raise a hand. When I see two people with hands raised, I'll call out, "Stop!" All individuals should freeze where they are.

I'll ask the two people with their hands up to simultaneously point to the Overdoser. If they point to two different people, both the accusers must fall down and die from an overdose. If they point to the same person who isn't the Overdoser, the accusers must also fall down as victims of an overdose. If they point to the correct person, the game is over. If they don't identify the correct overdoser, I'll ask you to mingle again until the Overdoser is identified.

Allow at least five minutes for this game. Then say: **To overdose is when you take more than a safe amount of any drug. During this meeting, we're going to discover the meanings of more words concerning drug use and abuse. We'll see how much we know about drugs, and we'll discover and discuss God's guidelines about drug use.**

2 Crossword capers
Say: **I'm going to give you a chance to test how much you know about drugs. I'll say a word, then you raise your hand if you think you know the description.**

Say these words:
★ Marijuana
★ Caffeine
★ Abstinence
★ Intoxicated
★ Overdose
★ Nicotine
★ Addiction
★ Alcohol

After kids attempt to define these words, say: **Good try with the descriptions. Let's check and see if we were right. I'll give each of you a crossword puzzle and pencil. Get with the person sitting closest to you and see if you can complete it. All of the words we tried to define are on the crossword puzzle.**

Allow several minutes for kids to work the puzzle. Then discuss the terms and definitions. Here are the answers for the crossword puzzle:

Down
1. Nicotine
3. Intoxicated
4. Caffeine
6. Alcohol

Across
2. Addiction
5. Marijuana
7. Abstinence
8. Overdose

3 A moral in a message
Ask partners to try to use all of the words from the crossword puzzle and create a message with a moral, or lesson, to read to the rest of the group. For

example: "*Drugs* are dangerous. Don't get *intoxicated* and definitely don't *overdose*. The use of drugs can lead to *addiction*. Whether the drug is *marijuana*, *alcohol*, *nicotine* or even *caffeine*, it can be dangerous. *Abstinence* is the way to avoid the dangers of drugs."

4 Bible views

Give partners a Bible and a "What Does the Bible Say?" handout. Assign each pair one of these passages:

★ Deuteronomy 29:2-6;
★ Luke 1:11-17;
★ 1 Corinthians 10:31-33;
★ Ephesians 5:15-20.

Let kids complete the handout according to what their verses say. Then have pairs report their findings.

5 Blackboard brainstorm

Draw a line down the center of the board. Label one side "Reasons to Take Drugs"; label the other side "Alternatives to Taking Drugs." Give kids a few minutes to brainstorm for each column. For example, a reason to take drugs could be to be accepted; an alternative could be to choose friends who have similar values.

6 Situation simulation

Have kids form five small groups, then give each group one of the situations from the "Situation Simulation" handout. Have the groups decide how a person in this situation could say no to the drug and still keep friends. If they get stuck, they can look at the board for some alternative ideas to using drugs.

Ask the groups to role play their situation to the large group. After the situation role plays, talk about other ways to not give in to pressure to use drugs. Offer these ideas and let kids add their own:

★ Take time to make a good decision.
★ Say no and keep saying no.
★ Talk about something else.
★ Ignore a request that doesn't seem right.
★ Tell a funny joke or story.
★ Say it's not right for you.
★ Offer an alternative.
★ Say you have to leave.
★ Find an excuse to stop talking.
★ Use your parents as an excuse.

★ Use your beliefs as an excuse.

★ Think of saying no to drugs as saying yes to yourself.

7 Thanks, God!

Gather kids in a circle for a closing "Thanks, God!" prayer. After each line you say, have kids repeat the line "Thanks, God!"

Thanks, God!

Leader: God, you've made each of us special and unique.

All: Thanks, God!

Leader: You've given us wonderful bodies to use for your glory.

All: Thanks, God!

Leader: You've given us the intelligence to make healthy decisions regarding drugs.

All: Thanks, God!

Leader: You've given us awareness, understanding and an ability to think how we can help ourselves, friends and family members avoid drug abuse.

All: Thanks, God. Amen!

Test Your Knowledge About Drugs

Clues

Across

2. Physical dependence on a drug.

5. A drug commonly called "grass," "pot" or "reefer."

7. When you choose not to use drugs.

8. To take more than a safe amount of any drug.

Down

1. The active ingredient in all forms of tobacco. Very addictive.

3. Being under the influence of a drug.

4. This drug can be found in coffee, cola and chocolate; it's a stimulant and can be addictive.

6. The #1 drug choice of young people and adults. It's a depressant.

What Does the Bible Say?

Instructions: Read your assigned scripture passage and answer the following questions.

1. What does the Bible say about a person's body?

2. What does the Bible say about wine or strong drink?

3. What guideline for using wine or strong drink does the Bible offer?

4. How can you use this guideline in your decision-making concerning drug use?

5. How can you use this guideline to help your friends make good decisions about drug use?

Situation Simulations

★ *Situation #1*—You and your best friend are at a party. She suggests that the two of you get some beer from the kitchen. You don't want to drink and you don't think your friend really does either. What do you do?

_____

★ *Situation #2*—A popular guy invites you to a party where you're sure there'll be lots of alcohol and drugs. You don't do that kind of stuff, and you're not sure whether the guy does. What do you do?

_____

★ *Situation #3*—You're at your best friend's house. When you and your friend go into the family room, his parents offer you some pot. Your friend takes a joint. What do you do?

_____

★ *Situation #4*—Your friend tells you she's been drinking her parents' liquor and replacing it with colored water. She wants you to stop over after school and try some. What do you do?

_____

★ *Situation #5*—You're on the playground before school. A person you'd like to be good friends with suggests the two of you smoke a cigarette before you go inside. What do you do?

PART 3:

My Relationships

By Rick Lawrence

What Kind of Friend Am I?

There's one school subject elementary kids can't afford to fail—friend-making. According to a study by the Journal of Child Psychology and Psychiatry, peer groups have a growing influence in the lives of today's kids. Much of kids' self-esteem grows out of the relationships they establish in class and on the playground.

Gisela Konopka, founder of the Center for Youth Development and Research, says: "School is seen by practically all kids as the major formal institution where they can find friends . . . Friendships with both sexes, intensified by growing sexual maturity, are exceedingly important—and complex; they demand decision-making about oneself, about others, about the present and the future."

Kids' early friendships are a testing ground for some important life lessons: trust, loyalty, honesty, forgiveness and unconditional love. Through trial and error with their friends, kids each form an identity that they'll carry with them the rest of their lives.

Objectives

In this meeting, upper-elementary kids will:

★ learn how they form and keep their friendships;

★ discover qualities that attract friends to one another;

★ experience attitudes and actions that can destroy friendships;

★ learn how Bible characters reacted to difficult friendship decisions; and

★ understand God's pattern for friendship and ask him for help in making and keeping friends.

Preparation

Read the meeting and photocopy the "Friendly Forest" handout. Gather colored markers, balloons, string, pencils, Bibles and a box of toothpicks.

Kids will need to write on building blocks. Find a supply of old toy building blocks, or you could make your own by using the following pattern.

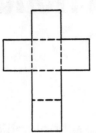

The Meeting

1· Building blocks of friendship

Form teams of three by having kids each hook elbows with two other people. Give each team three blocks, and give each person a toothpick. Have all teams line up at one end of the room.

Say: Each team has three blocks. The goal of this game is to stack your three blocks on top of each other at the other end of the room. It sounds easy, but here's what will make it hard: You're not allowed to touch the blocks with your hands. As a team, you must use your toothpicks to pick up, carry and stack your three blocks.

Each team member has been given one toothpick. Your team may choose to have one person carry the blocks using all the toothpicks. Or you may choose to involve everyone, with each person holding up part of the block using his or her toothpick. You'll have one minute to decide on your strategy; then I'll say "Go." The winning team is the first to successfully stack its three blocks at the other end of the room.

After you declare a winner, form a circle. Ask:

★ Did your team decide to use everyone to carry the blocks? Why or why not?

★ If you used everyone, would you have felt more confident carrying the blocks by yourself? Why or why not?

★ If you carried the blocks by yourself, would you have felt more confident with others helping out? Why or why not?

Read aloud Proverbs 18:24. Ask:

★ Do you agree with this scripture passage? Why or why not?

★ How important is it to have a few close friends you can depend on? Explain.

Say: The way you treat your friends is far more important than the number of friends you have. If you have few friends and you'd like more, try improving the friendships you already have.

2 The many sides of friendship

Give kids each a building block and some colored markers. Say: On one side of the block, write your name. On another side, write the names of your best friends. On another side, write all the reasons you like your friends. On another side, write all the reasons they like you. On another side, draw a picture of something you and your friends love to do. On the last side, write one thing you would change about your friendships if you had the chance.

Have kids build a tower with their completed blocks. Write "Jesus" in large letters on another block. Place that block on the top of the tower. Then read aloud Proverbs 17:17 and John 3:16-17. Ask:

★ Do your friends love you at all times? Why or why not?

★ Do you always love your friends? Why or why not?

★ How does Jesus love his friends differently than you or I?

3 Balloon buddies

Give kids each a balloon, a piece of string and a marker. Have them blow up their balloons and tie them with string. Tell each person one of the following five keys to friendship and have him or her write that one key on his or her balloon. The keys are: loyalty, honesty, forgiveness, service and love.

Tie the finished balloons together and place them in a corner of the room. Say: The words you've written on your balloons—loyalty, honesty, forgiveness, service and love—are all important keys to good friendships. If you and your friends practice these things, you'll enjoy your friendships for years to come. But sometimes friends do things to one another that threaten the friendship. And just like a popped balloon, your friendship can explode and leave you with nothing.

Form the same teams you had for activity #1. Say: I'm going to read some buddy-busting situations. In each situation, one of the five keys to good friendships is broken. After I read the situation, your team should decide which friendship key has been broken, then send a team representative to pop the balloons that have that word written on them. For example, if I read a story about friends who lie to each other, you should send a team member to pop all the balloons that say "Honesty."

Your team will receive one point for every popped balloon. If you pop the wrong balloons, your team will lose one point for every wrong balloon popped. The team with the most points at the end of the game, wins.

Read each of these situations and wait for the balloon busters to accomplish their task. After each situation, talk about why that broken friendship key could damage or destroy the friendship.

★ *Situation #1 (Loyalty Buster)*—Mark and Darren are best friends. They do everything together. They particularly enjoy sports. Last fall, they both tried out for a little league football team. Mark made the team as a quarterback. But Darren got cut from the team because he was too slow. Soon Mark became very popular. He stopped asking Darren to do things with him. He hung around with the popular group at school. And he avoided Darren in the school hallways.

★ *Situation #2 (Honesty Buster)*—Jennifer and Talia tell each other everything. One day, Jennifer tells Talia that she secretly likes a boy in her math class. Talia promises not to tell anyone, but she spreads the secret around anyway. Eventually, everyone in Jennifer's math class is teasing her about her secret. Jennifer confronts Talia, but Talia says, "I didn't tell anyone!"

★ *Situation #3 (Forgiveness Buster)*—John gets a new bike for his birthday. He calls his friend Mike to go bike riding. While they're riding, Mike asks John to let him ride his new bike. John says, "All right, but be careful." But as Mike is turning a corner on the new bike, he hits a patch of sand and wrecks the bike. Mike's knees are skinned and his shirt is torn. John runs up to him, grabs his bike and screams, "I told you to be careful. You're not my friend anymore!"

★ *Situation #4 (Service Buster)*—Steve's got a big test coming up that he'd like to study for in the morning. But Steve has a newspaper route in the morning. So he asks his friend Scott to deliver the newspapers for him just this one time. Scott says he'd rather sleep in than help Steve with his paper route.

★ *Situation #5 (Love Buster)*—Jill and Debbie are so close, they're like sisters. They depend on each other during rough times. And they like spending time with each other during good times. But since they've been friends for a few years, Jill sometimes takes Debbie for granted. Soon, Debbie feels like Jill doesn't even care about her anymore.

4 The friendly forest

Say: All friends go through good times and bad times. Long-lasting friendships are strong because the friends learn to forgive and appreciate one another. But some friendships break up because we don't want to admit we're wrong, or because we're more concerned with ourselves than with our friend, or because we don't stick by our friend in tough times.

Give kids each a "Friendly Forest" handout, a Bible and a pencil. Say: There are many paths through the Friendly Forest. Each one ends at a Bible passage that shows how people in the Bible reacted differently to their friends. Start at the bottom and follow the path you would choose if you faced a similar situation. When you make it to a Bible passage on the edge of the forest, find and read the passage in your Bible.

After kids have had time to complete the handout, gather together. Ask for volunteers to read aloud the Bible passages they found on the "Friendly Forest" handout. (It's likely that not all the passages will be read by kids, so read aloud the remaining passages.) Ask: After listening to the stories of these biblical characters, how should friends treat one another if they want their friendship to last?

5 Block prayer closing

Ask kids to each find the block they wrote on in activity #2. Form a circle. Go around the circle asking kids to each say a short prayer about the one thing (listed on their block) they'd change about their friendships if they could. Close the prayer by asking God for help in making and keeping friends.

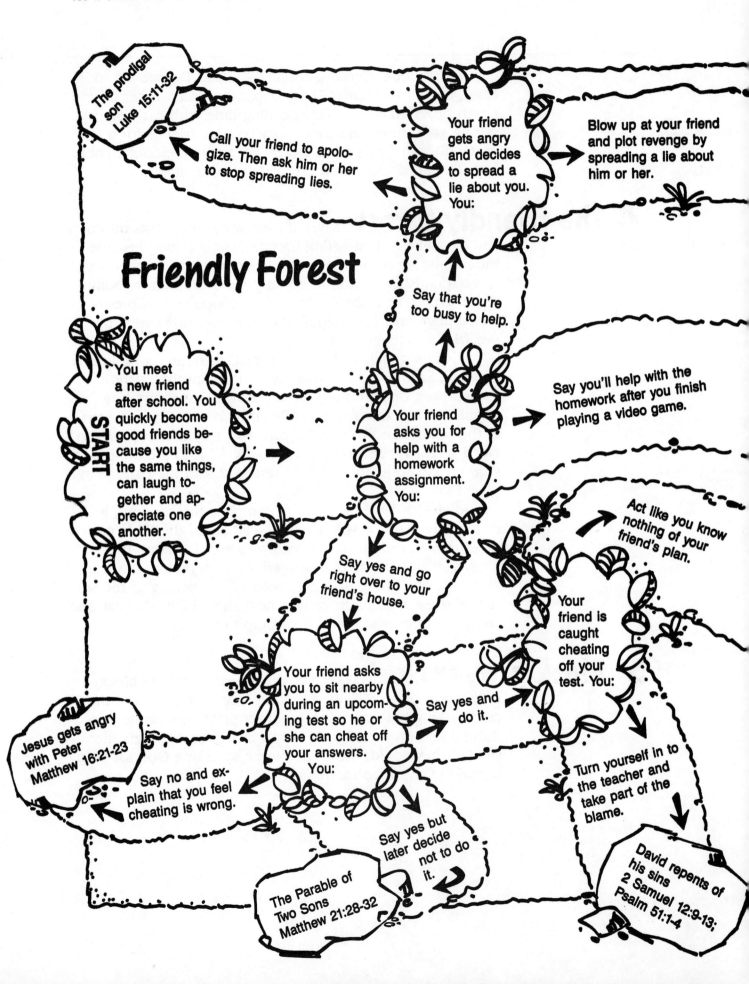

The prodigal son Luke 15:11-32

Call your friend to apologize. Then ask him or her to stop spreading lies.

Your friend gets angry and decides to spread a lie about you. You:

Blow up at your friend and plot revenge by spreading a lie about him or her.

Friendly Forest

Say that you're too busy to help.

You meet a new friend after school. You quickly become good friends because you like the same things, can laugh together and appreciate one another.

START

Your friend asks you for help with a homework assignment. You:

Say you'll help with the homework after you finish playing a video game.

Act like you know nothing of your friend's plan.

Say yes and go right over to your friend's house.

Your friend is caught cheating off your test. You:

Jesus gets angry with Peter Matthew 16:21-23

Your friend asks you to sit nearby during an upcoming test so he or she can cheat off your answers. You:

Say yes and do it.

Say no and explain that you feel cheating is wrong.

Turn yourself in to the teacher and take part of the blame.

Say yes but later decide not to do it.

The Parable of Two Sons Matthew 21:28-32

David repents of his sins 2 Samuel 12:9-13; Psalm 51:1-4

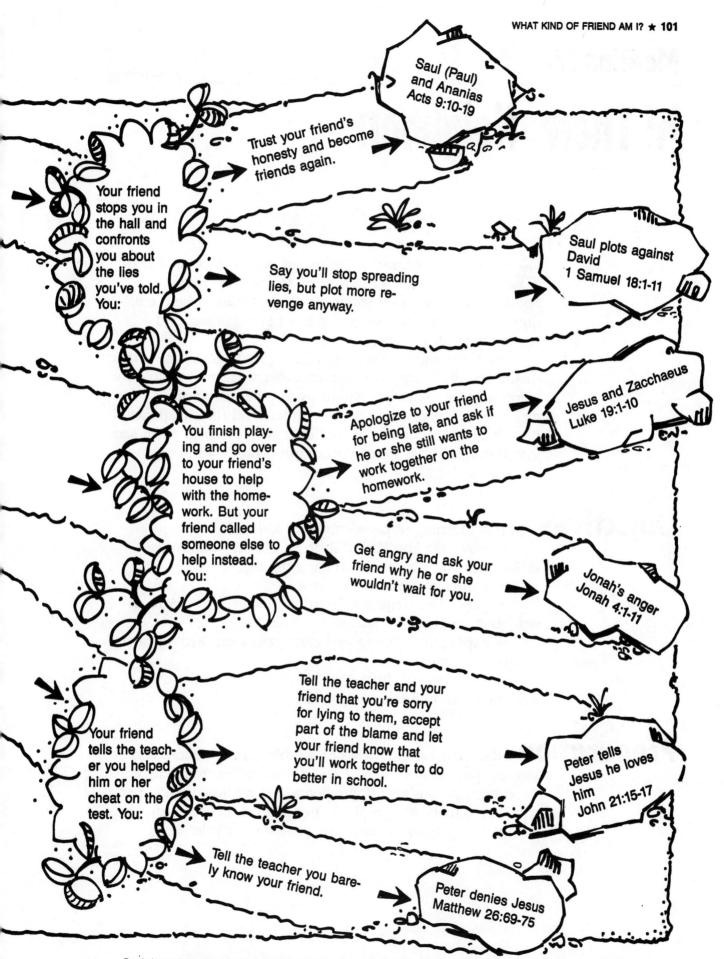

Saul (Paul) and Ananias
Acts 9:10-19

Trust your friend's honesty and become friends again.

Your friend stops you in the hall and confronts you about the lies you've told. You:

Say you'll stop spreading lies, but plot more revenge anyway.

Saul plots against David
1 Samuel 18:1-11

You finish playing and go over to your friend's house to help with the homework. But your friend called someone else to help instead. You:

Apologize to your friend for being late, and ask if he or she still wants to work together on the homework.

Jesus and Zacchaeus
Luke 19:1-10

Get angry and ask your friend why he or she wouldn't wait for you.

Jonah's anger
Jonah 4:1-11

Your friend tells the teacher you helped him or her cheat on the test. You:

Tell the teacher and your friend that you're sorry for lying to them, accept part of the blame and let your friend know that you'll work together to do better in school.

Peter tells Jesus he loves him
John 21:15-17

Tell the teacher you barely know your friend.

Peter denies Jesus
Matthew 26:69-75

Hi There, Neighbor!

An easily recognized voice in our world today is that of Fred Rogers, the #1 citizen of *Mr. Rogers' Neighborhood*. On his television show, Mr. Rogers tries to help children understand that our world is a big neighborhood where we're all citizens.

Jesus, through the parable of the good Samaritan, taught that everyone is our neighbor, and that we're responsible for helping one another. He taught us to love one another. This meeting will help young people understand their responsibilities to each other and our world. It will also help them see that through Christ we can accomplish much and become better neighbors.

Objectives

In this meeting, upper-elementary kids will:

★ play "Do You Know Your Neighbor?" and notice differences and similarities in each other;

★ participate in a melodrama;

★ play "The Neighbor Hunt" and learn how we're all neighbors in God's kingdom;

★ experience serving and caring through feeding each other refreshments; and

★ complete a "What Can I Do?" survey to discover how they can be better neighbors.

Preparation

Read the meeting. Gather a Bible, paper, pencils and photocopies of the "What Can I Do?" survey. You'll also need enough sandwich ingredients and drinks for each person. For activity #1, you'll need enough chairs for everyone except one person. Arrange the chairs in a circle.

The Meeting

1 Do you know your neighbor?

Tell the kids they're going to play a game to see how well they know other group members. Ask everyone to sit in a chair, except one person who'll stand in the center of the circle. The person who's in the center is "It." It walks up to anyone he or she chooses and asks, "Do you know your neighbor?" If that person answers "Yes," the two people seated beside him or her must swap seats while It also tries to get one of the seats. If the person answers "No," then he or she must continue by saying, "But I do know people who . . ." He or she concludes that phrase by listing a characteristic shared by several people in the circle. For example, "But I do know people who wear Nikes." The people wearing Nikes must change chairs while It also tries to get a seat. The person left without a chair becomes It.

After most everyone has had a chance to be It, stop the game and ask the kids to talk about some of the things they have in common.

2 It's not my job!

Say: We're now going to participate in a melodrama and learn who our neighbors really are. This melodrama is a script that'll be read by a narrator while others act it out. The actors will repeat the lines and follow the actions for their character as outlined by the narrator.

Choose kids for the parts. You'll need a narrator, Bubba (the victim), the Bully family (three robbers), Charlie Churchperson (a religious leader), Terry the Teacher (an educational leader), G. Samaritan (our heroine) and Dog (the dog).

The others can be the audience and boo and cheer at appropriate times. If you have fewer people than parts, decrease the number of robbers and combine other roles.

Introduce the melodrama by reading aloud Luke 10:29-37. Then say: Jesus let us know who our neighbor is by telling the parable of the good Samaritan. We're going to re-create a modern-day version of this parable.

It's Not My Job!

Our story opens on the road from a neighborhood elementary school to a nearby football field. Bubba, a typical, fun-loving student, has gone for a walk. As he walks along he can be heard whistling a happy tune. Then he begins to skip and jump. "What a great day!" he exclaims.

Just then three robbers, looking incredibly mean, jump out from behind a tree. "Oh no!" shouts Bubba. "I saw you last week in the principal's office."

"That's right!" the robbers exclaim in unison. "We're the Bully family—Bully #1, #2 and #3!" With that, they begin to beat up poor Bubba. Bully #1 kicks him. Bully #2 hits him. Bully #3 taunts him, "Nah-nah-nah-nah-nah, nah!" They take his lunchbox and go, leaving Bubba half-dead in the gutter.

A few minutes later, a local religious leader, Charlie Churchperson, happens down that same road. He sees Bubba lying in the gutter and says, "Oh dear. There's someone who needs help." He walks a little closer and sees that Bubba is in bad shape. "I can't help him," he says. "I might get my hands dirty." So Charlie Churchperson moves to the other side of the road and says, "It's not my job!" (The audience boos!)

A few moments later, along comes another leader, Terry the Teacher. She sees Bubba and thinks, "Boy, he's in bad shape." She pauses for a few seconds and then crosses to the other side of the road saying, "It's not my job!" (The audience boos!)

The next person to come along is a student from a rival elementary school, heading for home with her dog—a huge Saint Bernard. This student's name is G. Samaritan, and her dog's name, curiously enough, is Dog. Soon, G. Samaritan sees Bubba by the road and realizes right away Bubba needs help. Now students from these two schools don't like each other at all. But that doesn't matter to G. Samaritan. "This guy needs help," she says. "It's my job to take care of him!" (The audience cheers!)

She puts her coat over Bubba and puts him on her dog, Dog. They carry Bubba to the nearest Holiday Inn, and G. pays them to take care of Bubba and call his parents.

The Bully family is caught eating Bubba's lunch and is sent to the principal's office once again. Bubba survives and loves to tell people how he was rescued by G. Samaritan. "I know that G. stands for Good," says Bubba. G. Samaritan has shown what being a good neighbor is all about!

 3 The neighbor hunt Give each young person a piece of paper and a pencil. Have kids each write "Who Is My Neighbor?" across the top of their sheet, and then write on their sheet the name of someone who lives near them. As a group, decide on a definition of "neighbor." Then let the young people mingle, collecting signatures on their sheet from as many other young people as possible. After a few minutes, stop and discuss why every name represents a neighbor in God's kingdom. Explain that we're all brothers and sisters in God's family. Have kids look back at their definition of neighbor and see if it needs changing.

4 Feed me!

Read aloud Mark 12:29-31. Say: Shake the hand of somebody standing close to you. You two are partners.

Make sure no one is left out. Then explain that for refreshments, the partners will each make a sandwich and drink for each other and then feed each other.

After everyone has finished, discuss these questions:
★ What does it feel like to depend on someone else?
★ In what situations do we need each other?
★ In what situations do we need God?

5 What can I do?

Read aloud 1 John 4:7-8, then distribute the "What Can I Do?" surveys. After group members finish, discuss their answers. Emphasize how special each person is and how much of a difference we can make to all of our neighbors. Tell the young people to take their surveys home as reminders to be good neighbors.

Reread aloud 1 John 4:7-8. Then close your meeting with prayer, asking God to help your kids do what they can for others.

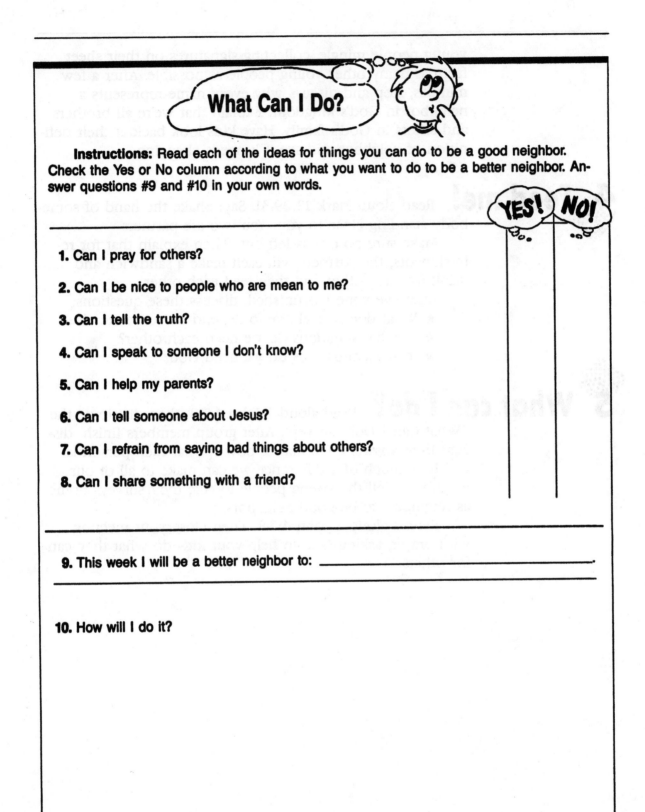

What Can I Do?

Instructions: Read each of the ideas for things you can do to be a good neighbor. Check the Yes or No column according to what you want to do to be a better neighbor. Answer questions #9 and #10 in your own words.

YES!   NO!

1. Can I pray for others?

2. Can I be nice to people who are mean to me?

3. Can I tell the truth?

4. Can I speak to someone I don't know?

5. Can I help my parents?

6. Can I tell someone about Jesus?

7. Can I refrain from saying bad things about others?

8. Can I share something with a friend?

9. This week I will be a better neighbor to: _____.

10. How will I do it?

Meeting 17

By Cindy Hansen

Those Super Spectacular Parents

Families are busier than ever with job responsibilities and school activities. In the rush, rush, rush of everyday life, it's easy to overlook the people who are most important to us.

Use this meeting to give upper-elementary kids a chance to take some time to think of all the reasons they appreciate their parents. Kids will also make a gift to give their parents to show their appreciation. Parents will be surprised and kids will feel good about showing their parents they care.

Objectives

In this meeting, upper-elementary kids will:
★ make a surprise sack of affirmations for their parents;
★ discuss the good qualities of their parents;
★ realize how much parents do for them; and
★ thank God for their parents.

Preparation

Read the meeting. Make S-shape name tags from construction paper. Gather pencils, paper, two blankets, "My Amazing Superparent" and "Power-Packed Promise" handouts, *Superman* theme song and a record or tape player, red yarn, construction paper, glue, scissors, sacks and magazines.

Ask two kids to advertise the meeting during announcement time in church. Dress one student in a football helmet and shoulder pads, jogging shoes and an apron. Have him or her wait by the door leading into the worship area. Ask another elementary student to introduce the waiting "actor" by exclaiming:

"Look! Out by the doorway! It's a bird! It's a plane! No! It's Superparent!"

(Enter the actor.)

"Yes, folks, it's Superparent. Able to cook meals with a flick of the microwave switch (actor wipes hands on apron), able to drive anywhere at a moment's notice (actor pantomimes driving), able to shoulder life's bumps and thumps (actor pantomimes a football block), able to run kids anywhere (jog in place). All upper-elementary students, come to our meeting this week at (time and place). We'll discuss more about our super, amazing parents and the spectacular things they do for us." ("Superparent" hauls off the announcer and says: "Come on, Junior. It's time to do your homework.")

The Meeting

1 Super name tags

Give kids each an S-shape name tag and have them write their name on it. Give them a minute or two to mingle, introduce themselves to each other and tell a super nice thing their parents did for them this week.

2 Superparent cape ride

Divide the group into two teams by having each one say either "Super" or "Parent." All "Supers" form one team; all "Parents" form another. Have each team form a line and choose one person to be the "Superparent" of their team.

Place a blanket at the front of each line. Each blanket represents Superparent's cape. Have the team members take turns sitting on the cape. Have the Superparent haul them, one at a time, up to a line and back. If you have more than five kids per team, designate one Superparent for every three kids. The first team to have all of its members "hauled" by its Superparent wins.

Say: Our meeting today is about our super parents and the good things they do for us. Just like the Superparents in our game, parents support us, urge us on during tough times, care for us, and help us meet life's goals. We're going to talk about the super things our parents do for us. By the end of this meeting we'll have a sack of surprises to give them to show how much we really appreciate them.

3 Superparent station rotation

Explain that the kids will form five small groups and rotate to different stations. At each station they will make something to affirm their parents. At the end of the rotation they will have completed a surprise sack for their parents.

Divide the group into five stations by having each person say one letter of "S-U-P-E-R" as the word is spelled out. All "S's" go to the first station, all "U's" go to the second station, and so on. (If you have a small group, instead of dividing and rotating, simply complete each station together.) If you divide into small groups, have a high school youth group member at each station.

Allow 10 minutes at each station. When it's time to rotate, have kids leave their creations at the station. Play the *Superman* theme song to signal the rotation time.

★ *Station #1 (Superparent Scroll)*—Tell kids that Superman was "faster than a speeding bullet, more powerful than a locomotive, and able to leap tall buildings in a single bound." Tell the kids they're now going to be able to describe the amazing feats of their Superparent.

Give each person a "My Amazing Superparent" handout and a pencil. Ask the kids each to fill in the blanks to describe their Superparent. After kids each complete their handout, have them roll it up in a "scroll" and tie it with a piece of red yarn.

★ *Station #2 (Superparent Symbol)*—Read aloud Proverbs 1:8-9. Give each person a piece of construction paper and scissors. Have kids each cut out a symbol of some advice their parent has told them. For example, a person could cut out a "smiley face" to represent the advice to give a smile away to cheer someone's day.

★ *Station #3 (Super, Power-Packed Promise)*—Say: Exodus 20:12 tells us to honor and respect our father and mother. One way we can respect and honor our parents is to show them we care by helping out around the house.

Distribute the "Power-Packed Promise" handouts and have kids each complete one for their parents.

Parent
Super parent
Super, nice parent
Super, nice, caring parent
Super, nice, caring, thoughtful parent
Parent
Thanks for all you do for me.

★ *Station #4 (Spectacular Add-a-Word Poems)*—Say: The more and more you think about it, the more and more you appreciate your parents. You're going to make an "add-a-word" poem where you start out with one word and add a word each line. Each word you add affirms your parent.

Distribute paper and pencils and let the poets create their masterpieces. Show them the example.

★ *Station #5 (Super Sack Decoration)*—Supply sacks, magazines, glue and scissors. Have kids each design a sack to symbolize the good qualities of their parents. For example, a student could decorate a sack with pictures of sports for an athletic parent. Take time to discuss the designs and how they symbolize their parents' good qualities.

4 Super sack stuffers
After kids have completed the rotations, have them get their decorated sacks. Play the *Superman* theme song one more time while kids go around to the stations, collect all their creations and stuff their sacks.

Gather kids in a circle for a closing prayer: God, thanks for super parents who are there for us when we need them. Help us to honor and appreciate them all the days of our lives. Thanks for parents' advice, wisdom, love and care. Amen.

Have kids give their sacks of affirmations to their parents when they go home.

5 Super variation
Plan a special time for parents like a "Soup"er Supper. Serve stupendous soup, crunchy crackers, powerful punch and rock 'em rolls. After the meal, sponsor an awards presentation for kids to give their spectacular sacks to their spectacular parents.

Power-Packed Promise

To: _____

I promise to: _____

I love you because: _____

From: _____

My Amazing Superparent

My Amazing Superparent's Name: _____

Faster than a _____

More powerful than a _____

Able to _____

Look!

Right in my own family!

It's a wonder!

It's a friend!

It's Superparent!

Super Seal of Approval

By Margaret Hinchey

Stamp Out Peer Pressure

"Those fifth- and sixth-graders have a lot more peer pressure than we do," reports eighth-grader Matt about his younger siblings. "By the time you're in junior high, you figure out that you don't have to do what everybody else does in order to be popular."

Matt's insight is borne out in surveys done by Search Institute, leading researchers of early adolescents. Although only 11 percent of those surveyed in grades five through nine admitted their friends "often" or "very often" try to get them to do things that are wrong, 15 percent of the fifth-graders and eight percent of the ninth-graders acknowledged influences of negative peer pressure.

When asked to list the areas of peer pressure they remembered in grades five and six, Matt and a half-dozen of his friends created the following list:

★ Cheating on tests or homework in school
★ Lying to parents
★ Shoplifting
★ Drinking
★ Smoking cigarettes
★ Stealing (money or other items in places other than stores)
★ Beating up someone
★ Vandalizing
★ Smoking marijuana or using other drugs

Once again, statistics support at least part of the "experience" of these young reporters. A recent survey of 100,000 readers of the elementary-age publication, Weekly Reader, reports that peer pressure to try beer, wine or liquor is on the increase since 1983, while pressure to try marijuana has experienced a decline during that time. An alarming 51 percent of the sixth-graders surveyed report that they receive pressure to try alcoholic beverages and 34 percent of that same group receives pressure to try marijuana.

The pressure's on!

Objectives
In this meeting, upper-elementary kids will:

★ see available choices and influences in various aspects of their lives;

★ discover tools to help them with their choices in life decisions;

★ role play different situations they may experience in the future; and

★ mold sugar cookie shapes and discuss the pressure to conform.

Preparation
Read the meeting. Each young person will need a pencil, a copy of the "Top Options to Pressure Points" handout, two balloons, two 12-inch pieces of string and a black marker. You'll need an item to symbolize "good," such as a test paper with an A on it or a Bible, and an item to symbolize "bad," such as an empty beer bottle or pack of cigarettes. You'll also need a blackboard and chalk or newsprint and a marker.

Consult a cookbook and find a sugar cookie recipe for the refreshment time. Prepare sugar cookie dough for kids to mold and bake sugar cookies.

Write on three slips of paper the options for responding to role play situations in activity #3. Place them in a basket.

Choose a meeting space that is familiar and comfortable to the youth—maybe the youth room or a classroom which they have used frequently. The space needs to be warm and inviting in order to engender honesty and forthrightness on the part of the youth. The room should also have four identifiable corners with space to stand in each corner.

Some of the situations discussed during this meeting may be very real to students in the class. Kids may be eager or hesitant to share their experiences. Remind the class of confidentiality if someone does disclose sensitive information.

The Meeting

1. Four corners
The purpose of this crowdbreaker is to begin the process of making choices. Tell the kids that you'll read four choices and assign one corner of the room for each

choice. They'll choose their favorite item by going to the designated corner. Remind them not to be influenced by peer pressure, but to go to their honest choice—not the one more of their friends have chosen.

Stand in the middle of the room (possibly on a chair in order to speak above the commotion). Start with one category, such as "Favorite School Subject." Point to one corner and say: This corner is for people whose favorite subject is math.

Point to the next corner and say: This corner is for people whose favorite subject is science.

Point to the next corner and say: This corner is for people whose favorite subject is social studies.

Point to the fourth corner and say: This corner is for people whose favorite subject is gym.

Continue to explain: On "go," proceed to your corner, introduce yourselves to each other and say why you chose this corner.

Allow 30 seconds of discussion, then move on to the next set of choices. Use these choices and make up more to fit your group:

Favorite School Subject
Math
Science
Social Studies
Gym

Favorite Food
Steak
Pizza
Lobster
Hamburgers

Favorite Room in Your House
Your bedroom
The bathroom
The kitchen
The family room

Favorite Family Vacation
Going to Disneyland
Going to the beach
Going to Grandma's
Skiing in Colorado

Favorite Season
Fall
Winter
Spring
Summer

Favorite Spectator Sport
Basketball
Football
Golf
Baseball

2 You're getting warmer

Tell the kids they're going to participate in another activity that has to do with choices and peer pressure. Ask one group member to go out of the room to a place where he or she can't hear or see what is going on. (Send an adult with the student in order to keep the student occupied.) After the young person has left, divide the group in two by numbering off. All "Ones" will be the negative peer pressure group. Give this group an empty beer bottle or pack of cigarettes. All "Twos" will be the positive peer pressure group. Give this group a test paper with an A on it or a Bible. Keep both groups intermixed; don't have two separate groups. Ask someone from each group to hide the representative item someplace in the room as the others from that group watch. Everyone needs to know where the items are except the person who's absent from the room. Make sure the two items are not in close proximity to each other. The items also need to be well hidden.

Bring in the absent volunteer and tell him or her that the task is to listen to peer guidance and try to find a hidden item. The volunteer has to decide who's leading in the right direction. The other kids can only say, "You're getting warmer" if the volunteer gets closer to their item or "You're getting colder" if the volunteer goes farther away from their item. Each group tries to lead the volunteer to their item. Who will win? Beware! The shouting and enthusiasm are contagious.

After one of the items is found, discuss these questions:

★ How did you feel about trying to lead someone to something negative? positive?

★ Would you have been more or less enthusiastic if you had been in the other group? Explain.

★ What made the volunteer decide to go with the directions of certain people?

★ How did it feel to have people yelling different directions?

3 Situation role play

Divide the group into three smaller groups by having them count off again. Place the basket with the three pieces of paper in the center of the room. The following statements should be on the pieces of paper:

★ Avoid the temptation and walk away from the situation without saying anything.

★ Go along with the temptation so that you aren't considered weird.

★ Ignore the temptation and stand up for what you know is right.

Have a spokesperson from each group choose one of the pieces of paper so that each group has a different role-play option for the following situations.

Read Situation #1 to the groups. Ask them to take about a minute to decide how they'd respond to the situation according to the option on their piece of paper. Have each group role play their response to the situation. After the role plays ask these questions:

★ Which option seemed most difficult to actually carry out? Why?

★ What other ways could we respond to this situation?

Follow this same procedure for each situation. Use these situations or make up your own:

★ *Situation #1*—You have a math test in sixth period. The guy who sits across the aisle from you doesn't understand math at all. He and several of his buddies meet you on the playground before the test to make a deal with you. They promise to give you $10 if you hold your paper so the guy across the aisle can see it during the test. What do you do?

★ *Situation #2*—You're responsible for babysitting your twin brother and sister who are 8 years old. Your parents are gone for the evening and won't be home until after midnight. Three of your good friends come over to your house and ask you to walk down to the mall that's just five blocks down the street. Your brother and sister are already in bed and you'll be back before your parents come home. What do you do?

★ *Situation #3*—You're walking home from school with your best friend. You stop at a convenience market to play a video game. While you and your friend are playing the game, some older kids come up to you and ask you to walk down the last aisle of the store and pick up some items for them. (In other words, shoplift!) One of the guys even twists your arm behind your back as he is making the request. What do you do?

4 Top options Give the kids time to examine their own decision-making. Distribute the "Top Options to Pressure Points" handout so that everyone has a clear understanding of what the biblical options are. If time and interest allow, make a list on the blackboard or newsprint of most-used options. Talk about why certain options are more comfortable to use than others.

5 Popping pressure

Give each young person a marker, two balloons and two pieces of string. Have the kids blow up the balloons and attach string to them. On the outside of each balloon, have the students write the top peer pressures they struggle with, such as cheating, lying to parents, and so on.

After the balloons have been labeled, have the young people tie the balloons to each of their ankles with the string. Then give them permission to pop their friends' balloons only when they say to the wearer of the balloon, "I don't want you to be tempted by this again." Then they may stomp on the balloon and pop it for their friend. Let this craziness continue until all the balloons are popped.

6 Pressure prayer

Ask the group members to join hands in a circle for prayer. The prayer has two parts. You begin by saying: Help us to fight off the pressure to . . .

Have the young people complete the sentence with one or two words. Then go around again and say: Thanks, Lord, for . . .

Let the group members complete the sentence.

At the end of the prayer, have a group pressure hug to show support for one another.

7 Conforming cookies

Supply sugar cookie dough. Let kids mold it into shapes and bake the cookies. Discuss how we are "molded" or "conformed" by peer pressure. Although the dough needs to be prepared ahead of time, the baking time is brief and will provide some creative, edible treats for the group members.

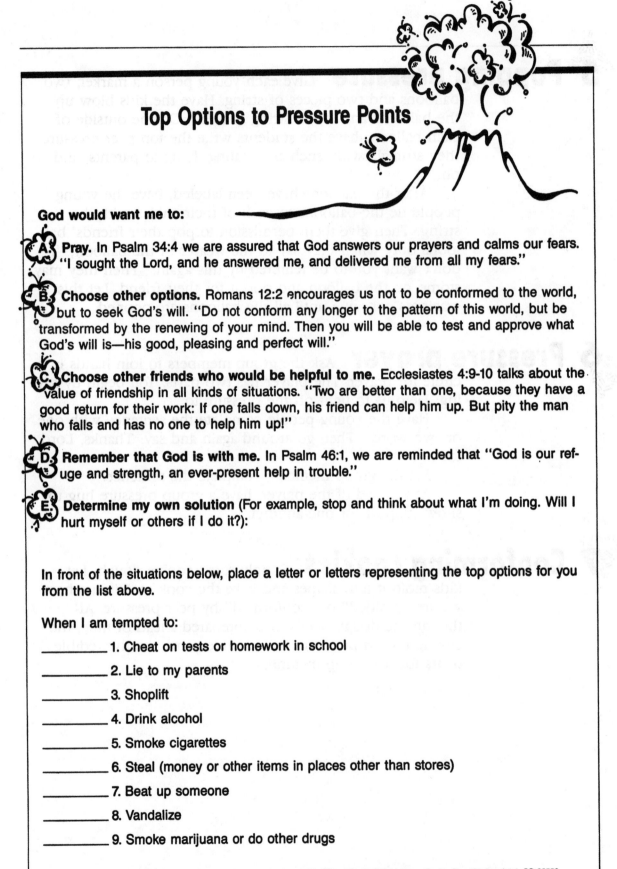

Top Options to Pressure Points

God would want me to:

A. **Pray.** In Psalm 34:4 we are assured that God answers our prayers and calms our fears. "I sought the Lord, and he answered me, and delivered me from all my fears."

B. **Choose other options.** Romans 12:2 encourages us not to be conformed to the world, but to seek God's will. "Do not conform any longer to the pattern of this world, but be transformed by the renewing of your mind. Then you will be able to test and approve what God's will is—his good, pleasing and perfect will."

C. **Choose other friends who would be helpful to me.** Ecclesiastes 4:9-10 talks about the value of friendship in all kinds of situations. "Two are better than one, because they have a good return for their work: If one falls down, his friend can help him up. But pity the man who falls and has no one to help him up!"

D. **Remember that God is with me.** In Psalm 46:1, we are reminded that "God is our refuge and strength, an ever-present help in trouble."

E. **Determine my own solution** (For example, stop and think about what I'm doing. Will I hurt myself or others if I do it?):

In front of the situations below, place a letter or letters representing the top options for you from the list above.

When I am tempted to:

_____ 1. Cheat on tests or homework in school

_____ 2. Lie to my parents

_____ 3. Shoplift

_____ 4. Drink alcohol

_____ 5. Smoke cigarettes

_____ 6. Steal (money or other items in places other than stores)

_____ 7. Beat up someone

_____ 8. Vandalize

_____ 9. Smoke marijuana or do other drugs

By Cindy Hansen

Care Packages for College Kids

Many times when young people from your church graduate from high school and leave for college, contact ends with them except for major holidays and summer vacation. Here's a meeting to use with your upper-elementary students to maintain caring contact with college kids. Upper-elementary young people will fill care packages with goodies for the college students. Use this idea at least twice a year— maybe more. Send care packages to show college kids your church is interested in them and cares for them even though they've moved on to new areas and interests.

Objectives

In this meeting, upper-elementary kids will:

★ hear Bible verses about service, reaching out, and Jesus's love and concern for us;

★ fill care packages with cookies, popcorn, cards and other goodies for college students; and

★ pray for God's protection and guidance in the college students' lives.

Preparation

Read the meeting. Gather Carefree sugarless bubble gum, ingredients and supplies for making cookies and popcorn, clear-plastic wrap, plastic sandwich bags, construction paper, markers, cardboard boxes, and tape and brown paper for wrapping the boxes.

Ask several kids to help you gather McDonald's coupons (or coupons from other fast-food restaurants) and church newsletters. Many churches enlist a person to record the pastor's sermons. If so, contact this person and get a cassette tape of a recent sermon. Make copies for each college student. Otherwise, arrange for an upper-elementary student and his or her parent to tape a sermon and make copies.

Ask your church office to supply a list of all college students' names and addresses. Send care packages even to those students who may be living at home and attending a nearby college. These care packages show the older students that your church still cares for them, even though they have graduated from high school and may not presently be involved in the fellowship of the church.

The Meeting

 1 A carefree contest As kids come into the room, give each one a piece of Carefree sugarless bubble gum. Ask kids to mingle around the room while they're chewing their gum, asking at least five people what fun activity they've done this past week.

After a few minutes of mingling and munching, have a contest to see who can blow the biggest bubble. Award a pack of bubble gum to the best bubble blower. Say: **Although we've just had a carefree time playing a fun game, God doesn't want us to be carefree in reaching out to others. He wants us to lovingly care and serve. We're going to have a chance to reach out to a group of people from our church—the college students. We're going to show them we care and show them they have a special place in our church by sending them each a care package.**

2 Care-package crews Divide the group into smaller groups to make these care-package contents.

★ *Cookie Bakers*—Have a crew make cookies in the kitchen. This could be as simple as buying ready-made cookie dough, slicing and baking it. Wrap several cookies for each care package.

★ *Popcorn Poppers*—Let a small group pop popcorn, salt it, butter it and bag it.

★ *Fold-Out Form Folders*—Ask one group to fold 4×11 inch sheets of construction paper accordian-style. On the front of each form write, "A Fold-Out Form of Fun Thoughts From Your 'Fun'tastic Friends." Let everyone sign his or her name and add a fun thought or bit of advice such as, "If you're feeling down and blue, always remember we're praying for you." Kids could also write a favorite Bible verse such as John 3:16 or a note about a favorite Bible character. For example, "If you ever feel like you're going through a cloudy time, read about Noah in Genesis 6—9. God helped him through a major storm."

 **3 Care-package construction** After everyone has made these care-package goodies, form an assembly line. On a long table, place the cardboard boxes, McDonald's coupons, church newsletters, sermon tapes, bags of cookies, bags of popcorn and fold-out notes. Let each person grab a box and start filling it by proceeding down the assembly line. Wrap the boxes in brown paper, tape them and address them.

4 Care chorus Gather around the care packages and grab hands. Read the following Bible verses in the "Care Chorus" and encourage kids to repeat your last sentence after each one.

Care Chorus

Leader: Matthew 6:26 says: "Look at the birds of the air; they do not sow or reap or store away in barns, and yet your heavenly Father feeds them. Are you not much more valuable than they?" God cares for each one of us, and we care for others.
Response: God cares for each one of us, and we care for others.

Leader: 1 John 3:1 says: "How great is the love the Father has lavished on us, that we should be called children of God! And that is what we are!" God loves us, and we love others.
Response: God loves us, and we love others.

Leader: Matthew 20:26-28 says: "Whoever wants to become great among you must be your servant, and whoever wants to be first must be your slave—just as the Son of Man did not come to be served, but to serve, and to give his life as a ransom for many." Jesus served us, and we serve others.
Response: Jesus served us, and we serve others.

Say: Just as Jesus cares for us, loves us and shows us how to serve, we will care for others, love others and serve them. Let's offer a silent prayer asking God to guide, protect and care for the college students.

Clean up the area, eat any leftover goodies and delegate some group members to mail the packages!

5 Other package-packing ideas

★ Invite congregation members to send a note to each college student. After church one Sunday, have group members set up a table with a sign that says, "College Kid Contact Center." Have 3×5 cards and pencils available. Encourage members to write notes to the college kids on the 3×5 cards. Collect the cards and stuff the care packages with them.

★ Ask the church secretary to keep the college kids on your church's mailing list, so they receive your church newsletter and other mail on a regular basis.

★ Have group members send care packages on major holidays. For example, before Valentine's Day send each college person a custom-made card. Make cards from construction paper, ribbons, glitter, and so on. Let congregation members sign the cards, then mail them along with Valentine heart-shape candy or heart-shape sugar cookies.

★ Have kids send a care package to celebrate each college kid's birthday. A birthday care package could include a birthday card, cupcake, candle, small present such as a piece of fruit or a candy bar and a cassette tape with all the upper-elementary kids singing happy birthday.

By Denise Turner

Dealing With Divorce

A young girl invited her new friend to spend the night. The friend was amazed when she arrived with her overnight bag and found a mother, father and two children at home. "You mean you live with both of your real parents?" the friend asked in an awe-filled voice.

A commonly cited statistic is that half of today's new marriages will end in divorce. And it's estimated that 60 percent of today's children will spend part of their childhood in a single-parent family. To compound the problem, most young people feel they should hide their true emotions when their parents divorce. Many of the parents are under too much pressure to give their children the time and energy they require.

It's time for the church to address the subject of divorce. Especially when it comes to the innocent children who are often left alone to cope with this real issue in today's society. An upper-elementary meeting about divorce can be a tool to help not only the children of divorced parents, but also the children whose friends are being forced to cope with the problem.

Objectives

In this meeting, upper-elementary kids will:
★ learn about change and separation;
★ discover steps to handle loneliness and grief;
★ discuss opinions about divorce; and
★ write a letter to help clarify their thoughts.

Preparation

Read the meeting. Gather masking tape, paper, pencils, Bibles, markers, and a picture of a boy or girl clipped from a magazine. You'll also need enough empty cardboard boxes for kids to build a wall in the center of the room. If you want to participate in a taffy-pull, ask a parent to prepare the taffy and have it ready for refreshments at the end of the meeting.

Some of your group members may be experiencing or may have recently experienced a divorce in the family. Be especially sensitive to these children, taking every opportunity to help them see that anger and tears are valid and normal reactions to divorce. Help them understand that it's possible for them to work through their problems and lead happy lives. Listen closely to these children so you can respond with understanding.

The Meeting

1 Suffering separation
Show kids the empty boxes and masking tape. Tell them to tape the box flaps shut and build a wall in the center of the room.

Divide the group in two by having them count off by twos. All "ones" stand on one side of the wall of boxes; all "twos" stand on the other side. Distribute markers to everyone, then say: Today's meeting is about divorce. Divorce is a loss. Divorce makes you sad and lonely. Divorce is a separation. Although we might not have experienced a divorce, a lot of us have experienced separation. How many of you were ever separated or lost from your parents?

Take your markers and write on the box wall as many situations as you can that have to do with separation or loneliness; for example, moving to a new city, being left with a new babysitter, the first day of school, the death of a pet, the death of a grandparent, and so on.

After kids have had time to write on the wall, talk about the separation and lonely times.

2 Handling loneliness and separation
Say: All of these times cause us sadness and grief. When people are separated from loved ones in times like these, they go through several steps of grief. The first step is denial, or the "I can't believe it" way of handling loneliness. Everybody put your hands over your ears and say, "I can't believe it."

The next step is emptiness. The person doesn't feel like doing anything. Put your hands on your stomach, look lonely and say, "I'm empty."

The next step is anger, or lashing out at someone. Everyone hit your hand with your fist and say, "I'm mad."

The final step is moving forward, moving beyond the intense time of grief and loneliness. Everybody walk three steps and say, "I'm moving on."

Divorce is another form of separation that involves a similar grief process. Let's repeat the steps.

After they repeat the steps to handling grief, ask:

★ Is divorce always bad for the children involved? Explain.

★ Can any good come out of a divorce?

★ Why does divorce happen?

★ Is there anything we can do to stop it? Explain.

3 Answers to questions

Divide the group into four smaller groups by having the two previous groups divide in half. Provide each group with a pencil, piece of paper and a Bible. Instruct each group to think of five questions a child might ask about divorce. Have one person in each group write down the questions. Questions could include:

★ Is it a child's fault when parents divorce?

★ Does God forgive people when they divorce?

★ How do you get over bad feelings?

Allow 10 minutes for groups to work. Then instruct groups to switch lists of questions and, using their Bibles as necessary, discover ideas God has for answering these questions. Try these verses:

★ Psalm 130:4; Matthew 6:15; and Mark 11:25 (Forgiveness)

★ Matthew 6:25-34 (Don't worry)

★ John 14:27 (God's peace)

Allow another 10 minutes. Then discuss the questions and answers. Follow this with questions such as:

★ Who should a child talk with if he or she is afraid his or her parents might be heading toward a divorce?

★ Is there anything a child can do to stop trouble between his or her parents? Why or why not?

4 Continuum opinions

Make sure everyone is on one side of the box wall. Say: These boxes are now a scale. The right end means "Absolutely yes." The left end means "Absolutely no." The middle means "I don't know." I'll read some situations. You go stand by the point on the scale that best represents your thoughts. We'll discuss our opinions after each situation. Use these thoughts and add others.

Allow time for kids to move to a point on the scale and discuss their opinions after each thought.

★ A husband and wife who fight a lot always end up divorced.

★ Divorce is always wrong.

★ Kids shouldn't feel guilty if their parents divorce.

★ The best way to help a friend whose parents are divorcing is to tell him or her to forget all about it.

5 Letter writing
Show the group members a photograph of a boy or girl you clipped from a magazine. Explain: Imagine this young person's parents just got divorced. Some of you may never experience the divorce of your own parents. But most of you will someday need to help a friend whose parents are divorcing. I'll give you each some paper and a pencil. Write a short letter to this person. Try to make your friend feel better.

Afterward, read the letters.

6 Busting down walls
Have the group gather by the wall of boxes. Ask kids to think of things they're thankful for—things God has blessed them with. Say: God blesses us with many things. Even in the midst of lonely, sad times, we can look around and know that God is with us. He loves us and cares for us.

Ask kids to name their blessings. One at a time, with each blessing, take down a box. After the wall is dismantled say: God breaks down our walls of loneliness with blessings, with good friends who listen to us and hug us, with good parents who try to do what's best.

7 Taffy-pull
For refreshments you could have a taffy-pull and talk about the way lonely times try to pull us apart, but how God holds us together. Then eat the sticky sweets!

Contributors

Kathleen Boyd served as a volunteer youth leader in Pennsylvania. She passed away soon after submitting her meeting for publication.

Karen Ceckowski is media manager for Group Publishing. She also serves as a youth ministry volunteer and retreat coordinator in Colorado.

Cindy Hansen is an elementary schoolteacher in Colorado. She formerly served as managing editor of Group Books.

Margaret R. Hinchey is director of special events for Group Publishing.

Carl Jones is a director of youth ministries and Christian education in North Carolina.

Dr. Scott E. Koenigsaecker is an associate pastor in California with responsibility for youth ministries.

Rick Lawrence is assistant editor for GROUP Magazine.

Jim Reeves serves as a family therapist in Colorado. He's a former youth minister and counselor.

Linda Snyder is a director of youth ministries in Florida.

Tim Suby is a youth minister in Iowa.

Denise Turner is a writer in Idaho. She also leads seminars and workshops.

Terry Vermillion is a youth director in Missouri.

Paul Woods is managing editor of Group Books.

Practical Programming Resources
for Your Youth Ministry from

10-MINUTE DEVOTIONS FOR YOUTH GROUPS

By J.B. Collingsworth

Get this big collection of ready-to-use devotion ideas that'll help teenagers apply God's Word to their lives. Each 10-minute faith-building devotion addresses an important concern such as:

- love
- peer pressure
- failure
- rejection
- faith, and more

You'll get 52 quick devotions complete with scripture reference, attention-grabbing learning experience, discussion questions and a closing. Bring teenagers closer to God with these refreshing devotions—perfect for youth activities of any kind!

ISBN 0-931529-85-9 $5.95

BUILDING ATTENDANCE IN YOUR YOUTH MINISTRY

By Scott C. Noon

Now you can make your group grow—and learn what to do when it does! You'll get practical ideas for bringing new kids in the door, and design faith-building programs to keep them. Discover . . .

- Formulas for setting realistic goals
- Hints for planning long-term expansion
- Effective ways to handle growth

Whether you're just starting out or a youth ministry veteran, you'll get tools that really work—for building attendance in *your* youth group!

ISBN 0-931529-84-0 $10.95

BEATING BURNOUT IN YOUTH MINISTRY

By Dean Feldmeyer

Fight burnout, get more done, and still have time for your family and yourself. With this easy-to-read guide you'll discover practical, new ways to:

- Set realistic goals
- Eliminate time-wasters
- Learn when and how to say no
- Find time to recharge your creative batteries

Plus, you'll get helpful worksheets, revealing self-quizzes and loads of practical insights for both novices and pros. Take control of your schedule today with **Beating Burnout in Youth Ministry**.

ISBN 0-931529-47-6 $9.95

THE YOUTH MINISTRY RESOURCE BOOK

Edited by Eugene C. Roehlkepartain

Stay on top of youth ministry, young people and their world with the most complete, reliable and up-to-date resource book ever!

- Get the facts on today's teenagers
- Find out who's doing what in youth ministry
- Get the scoop on youth ministry salaries
- Discover resources galore!

Depend on **The Youth Ministry Resource Book** to help you plan youth meetings and retreats. Write newsletters. Prepare youth talks and sermons. Work with parents of teenagers and more. You'll find support for your ministry to young people with this handy gold mine of information.

ISBN 0-931529-22-0 $16.95